Beginner's
Ladino
WITH ONLINE AUDIO

BEGINNER'S
Ladino
WITH ONLINE AUDIO

ALLA MARKOVA

HIPPOCRENE BOOKS, INC.
New York

Audio files available at www.hippocrenebooks.com

Online audio edition, 2018.
Text copyright © 2008 Alla Markova
Audio copyright © 2008 Hippocrene Books, Inc.

For information, address:
HIPPOCRENE BOOKS, INC.
171 Madison Avenue
New York, NY 10016
www.hippocrenebooks.com

Previous edition ISBN: 978-0-7818-1225-2

Cataloging-in-publication data available from the Library of Congress.

ISBN 978-0-7818-1372-3

To the memory of my father, Meyer ben Faivus Alter Markov, an Ashkenazi Jew, who introduced me to Sephardic culture and encouraged my learning of Ladino.

Contents

Audio files available for download at:
http://www.hippocrenebooks.com/beginners-online-audio.html

Introduction

"No me importa ke nombre uzan para muestra lingua.
Lo importante es ke la avlen i ke la melden, i ke traten
de eskrivir letras, poezias, artikolos i livros en esta lingua
—porke solo de esta manera puedra kontinuar a bivir."

Moshe Shaul, Redaktor de la revista *Aki Yerushalayim*

"It does not matter to me what name is used for our language.
What matters is that people speak it, read it and try to write
letters, poetry, articles and books in this language—as only in
this way will it be able to keep on living."

Moshe Shaul, Editor of the magazine *Aki Yerushalayim*

HISTORY OF THE LADINO LANGUAGE

Ladino is one of the names used to designate the language of the
Sephardic Jews or Sephardim. It is also commonly known as *Judeo-
Spanish*, *Djudezmo* (*Judezmo*), *Haketia*, *Sephardic*, *Romance*, or
Spanyolit. In this book the term *Ladino* is used for consistency.

Every language reflects the history of its users. This is certainly true
of Ladino. The word *Sephardic* comes from *Sepharad*—the Hebrew
name for the Iberian Peninsula. The Jews who lived on the Iberian
Peninsula were extremely familiar with the host culture, as shown
by their knowledge of the Romance languages spoken by the popula-
tions of the region. Romance refers to a group of languages derived
from Latin. Jews both spoke and wrote in Romance languages, but
used their traditional writing system, Hebrew script. As Castilian
became more prevalent among the many Romance vernaculars spoken
in the region with the growing importance of Castile, many Jews
adopted it. After the Expulsion of the Jews in 1492, Sephardim in
the countries of the Diaspora preserved this language as part of their
Iberian heritage.

The language of the Sephardic Jews reflects their many wanderings. In 1492, some of those expelled emigrated south and eastward to North Africa and to various regions of the Ottoman Empire. About 70,000 Spanish Jews went west to neighboring Portugal. But only four years later, when all Jews, both Spanish and Portuguese, were forced either to accept baptism or to leave Portugal, tens of thousands more joined their brethren in various other parts of the Mediterranean.

This exodus led to the formation at the end of the fifteenth century of a new Diaspora of Jews whose spoken language was a number of Romance vernaculars including Old Castilian and Portuguese. When the Sephardim settled in the places inhabited by other Jews, they kept to themselves, forming their own communities and cherishing their Iberian legacy. For people to flee persecution is not surprising, nor is it surprising that they continued to speak the language of their former country for several generations. The unique phenomenon of the Sephardim is not only that they kept the language of their persecutors for more than half a millennium, but that they retained their nostalgic longing for the country that expelled them.

Generations and generations of Jews continued to use the linguistically archaic language (when compared to present-day Castilian or Portuguese) that their ancestors had brought from the Iberian Peninsula. While languages in Iberia continued developing and evolving, the Sephardim tried to preserve the fifteenth-century language of their forefathers. Despite this, it would be incorrect to refer to this language as *Old Spanish*. Changes in the surrounding world led inevitably to changes in the language. As more and more new words and grammatical categories made an appearance, some of the old ones began to disappear. Gradually, a new language was formed; its name, Ladino, identifies it as a Romance language, deriving from Latin.

As a language of Jews, Ladino was strongly influenced by Hebrew and adopted many Semitic words and phrases. The variant of Ladino used for the liturgy has numerous examples of literal translation, as well as grammatical features and syntax borrowed directly from Hebrew. This version is often called the Judeo-Spanish calque to distinguish it from the vernacular spoken language.

Since the Sephardim settled in many parts of the Mediterranean region and lived alongside various peoples, a number of different Ladino dialects were formed over time.

WRITING

While Jewish languages may be stateless, they nevertheless have a writing system; this is also so for Ladino. Many centuries before the Expulsion, when Ladino as such did not exist, Jews began using their traditional alphabet to write in Old Castilian. Moors and Jews, in fact, wrote in Old Castilian before Christians. The most ancient extant documents in Castilian are not written in Latin, but in either Arabic or Hebrew letters.

Since the Hebrew alphabet has only consonant letters, the Sephardim adapted it for writing in a Romance language. They used several Semitic consonant letters to designate vowels:

the letter *aleph* (א) is read as [a]
the sound [a] in final position in a word is usually designated by
    the letter *hei* (ה)
the letter *vav* (ו) can be read as [o] or [u]
the letter *yod* (י) reads as either [e] or [i]

In some cases, where the difference between [e] and [i] is important, the Hebrew diacritic sign *tsere* (two dots under the letter) is used to denote [e].

In some dialects of Ladino, unaccented o is pronounced as [u] and e as [i], as in modern Portuguese. Ladino script, by using only three vowels, helped to eliminate the dialectal difference between regions and made a written document understandable to any Ladino-speaking person.

SCRIPT TYPES

Sephardic Jews used square characters, but more common was the use of Rashi, another Hebrew script variant. Rashi is an acronym of the name of the eleventh-century Rabbi Shlomo Yitshaki, who was famous for his commentaries to the Talmud, which were originally copied and later printed in a script that became known as *Rashi*.

Rashi script was widely used in the Middle Ages and Early Modern period and many Hebrew *incunabulae* (the first printed books

before 1500) were printed in it. Since the Sephardim took the fonts
with them into exile and started printing presses in places where they
settled, book printing in the Ottoman Empire appeared much earlier
than in many Western countries. The oldest extant Hebrew *incu-
nabula* from Constantinople (Istanbul) dates to 1493, one year after
the Expulsion. In fact, for several centuries the only printing presses
in the Ottoman Empire were Jewish, as Muslims were prohibited
from printing the Quran.

Jews founded printing presses in Salonika (Thessalonika), Izmir
(Smyrna), and several other cities, as well as in the Ottoman capital, making books easily available in all regions. Since Rashi was
the most commonly used font, books in that script were printed in
both Hebrew and Ladino. This is why Sephardic cursive, sometimes
called *soletreo,* is based on the Rashi script and is very different from
the traditional Ashkenazic (Yiddish) cursive. In Spain, Ladino texts
written with any kind of Hebrew letters are called *aljamiado.*

A considerable number of books were printed in Ladino in the sixteenth and seventeenth centuries, not only in the Ottoman Empire,
but also in Italy. The printing press helped to spread a more-or-less
unified Ladino throughout the Mediterranean area and even to some
parts of Western Europe.

EASTERN SEPHARDIM

Although from the sixteenth century on, the majority of the Sephardim lived in one state—the Ottoman Empire—their linguistic
surroundings varied greatly. In Constantinople and Asia Minor, Jews
lived alongside Turks, Greeks, and Armenians; in the Balkans, the
host population was either Greek or Slavic; and in North Africa,
the language was Arabic. As always, pronunciation and vocabulary
were the first to change. Words and phrases from all of the languages
belonging to different linguistic groups entered the colloquial language of Jews. In Ladino the new borrowings became assimilated
by adapting appropriate gender, grammatical endings, and conjuga-
tional structure to them so that today only a specialist can distinguish
them from the original Castilian words. For example, the words
musafir (guest, traveler) and *alhad* (Sunday) come from Arabic; *asker*

(soldier) and *defter/tefter* (register) from Turkish; *papu* (grandfather) from Greek and *prvi* (first) from Croatian, etc.

Turkish influence was strongest, though in some areas it came to Jews through other languages, and a number of originally Arabic (i.e. Semitic) words came into Ladino from the Turks. At the same time, many Spanish or Portuguese words were lost or changed their meanings. Under the influence of local tongues, the pronunciation began to differ from that used by the Spaniards, and vary from region to region. And although many educated Sephardim continued to call their language Castilian, it became increasingly different from the language spoken in Castile.

WESTERN SEPHARDIM

While some Iberian Jews preferred expulsion to forced baptism, others stayed and converted to Christianity, joining the group of New Christians (*conversos* or *Marranos*) who had appeared in Castile after the pogroms and forced baptisms of 1391. The Inquisition, however, drove many New Christians to flee the Peninsula as soon as they were able to do so. While some, merely wanting to escape persecution, became sincere Catholics, others decided to return to the faith of their forefathers and settled in Amsterdam where they formed their own congregation.

Unlike their eastern brethren whose ancestors had never been baptized and who had continued to preserve Jewish education throughout the years, the Amsterdam Jews were ex-conversos. Most of them were literate and well-off, and because they had received a Christian education, spoke and wrote highly refined Spanish and Portuguese, but not Hebrew or Ladino. The Amsterdam Jews created Jewish schools and printing presses, and since the community experienced an ongoing influx of conversos from the Peninsula, printed books mainly in Portuguese and sometimes in Spanish for them.

Some of the ex-conversos remained in Western Europe, primarily in the Netherlands, but also in England and Germany; some later traveled to the New World. Many refugees, however, went to the Mediterranean area and settled in Italy and the Balkans where their Portuguese influenced the Ladino of local Jews.

The result of all of these migrations was the emergence of two main dialects of Mediterranean Ladino: the eastern one which preserved more features of Castilian and is spoken in Constantinople, Izmir, Rhodes, and Adrianopolis; and the western one, which has more elements of the Andalusian and Portuguese Romance languages and is found in Thessalonika, Bosnia, Macedonia, and Romania.

While the Sephardic communities of the sixteenth and seventeenth centuries flourished in the Mediterranean, by the eighteenth century they were on the decline in all areas of life, from the economic to the cultural. The number of printed titles diminished significantly, and the quality of printing deteriorated drastically. The cultural situation of Mediterranean Jews became so desperate that a special educational institution, the Alliance Israelite Universelle, was created by French Jews to provide assistance. Starting in 1860, the Alliance organized Jewish schools in many cities of the region. Instruction in the Alliance Universelle schools was in French, a language many wanted to learn and which became the language of the cultural elite; in this way numerous Gallicisms entered Ladino. Just as had been the case with Turkish, the French words acquired Spanish endings, and some of the original Spanish synonyms were forgotten. This is how words like *longe* (instead of *lejos*), *buto* (instead of *meta*), and *malorozamente* (instead of *desgraciadamente*) appeared.

From the beginning, the twentieth century was a tragic one for Sephardic Jews. In 1912, Thessalonika, a city whose population was predominantly Jewish and the most important cultural center of the Sephardim, known as the Jerusalem of the Balkans, became Greek. Reneging on its promises, the Greek government introduced discriminatory measures against Jews and their language, forcing many Jewish families to relocate to Turkey or to emigrate from the Balkans to the United States. In 1917, virtually the entire Jewish section of Thessalonika was destroyed by fire, and the flames extinguished not only human lives but also houses, synagogues, schools, and ancient manuscripts and books, including *incunabulae* brought centuries earlier by refugees from Spain. After the pogroms of 1931, some ten thousand Jews left Thessalonika for Palestine. In 1941, Greece was occupied by the Nazis who exterminated nearly all its Jews, and Thessalonika lost 96 percent of its Jewish population. Jews from other places in the Balkans, aside from Bulgaria, suffered the same fate.

After World War II, when the majority of Holocaust survivors opted to go to the United States or Palestine, the number of people speaking Ladino shrank along with its use. Recently, there has been a revival of interest in Ladino and in the history of its speakers, who have kept their language and traditions alive for more than five hundred years. In an effort to preserve the language, a number of universities have begun to include Ladino in their curricula. It will be the task of this new generation of Ladino speakers to provide both the language and its distinctive culture and history with a new lease on life.

CULTURAL CENTERS

Within the Mediterranean region, the Sephardim lived mostly in the port cities. Though after the Expulsion some settled in present-day Morocco, Algeria, and Tunisia, the overwhelming majority migrated further east where they were welcomed by the Ottoman Sultan Bayazid II. The Balkans had recently been conquered by the Turks, and Bayazid offered Jews certain privileges for settling in those lands and developing them for the Empire.

The greatest number of Jews went to Istanbul, the former Constantinople and capital of the Empire. It was the relatively unknown town of Thessalonika, however, that became the most important center of Sephardic culture. For more than four centuries, starting from the end of the fifteenth century until 1912, the Sephardim formed the majority of the city's population and their language was dominant, broadly used as a language of commerce by the non-Jewish population, including Greeks, Turks, Armenians, and Slavs. In the sixteenth century, Thessalonika became the center of Sephardic scholarship and of Jewish knowledge in general. The authority of the Thessalonikan rabbis was so great that Jews from all over the world sent their questions to them. The city was filled with schools, printing presses, and synagogues. Thessalonika (Saloniko in Judeo-Spanish) was called *la madre de Israel* (the mother of Israel) or *la Yerushalayim de los Balkanes* (the Jerusalem of the Balkans).

Other major centers of Sephardic culture were Izmir (Smyrna) in Asia Minor, Split and Dubrovnik (Ragusa) in the Balkans, Safed

(Tsfat) and Jerusalem in Erets Israel, Tetouan and Tangier in North Africa, and Leghorn (Livorno) and Venice in Italy.

MOST IMPORTANT WORKS

The book *Proverbios morales* (*Moral Proverbs*), 1351, by R. Shem Tov de Carrion is usually considered to be the oldest work in Ladino. Among other extant pre-Expulsion works, the best known are *Siddur Tefillot* (a prayer book for women), *Paraquim* (*Sayings of the Fathers*) in Latin script, and the *Takkanot de Valladolid* (*Communal Enactments of the Valladolid Community*), 1432.

Major creative activity in Ladino began after the Expulsion. In the first generation of Spanish Jews born outside of the Peninsula, the most important individual was R. Moshe Almosnino (1515 or 1518–1580). His book *Regimiento de la vida* (*The Management of Life*), 1564, Thessalonika, was a manual for living for new communities, explaining both what to do and what to read. It was so popular that in 1729 it was printed in Amsterdam in Latin script.

The masterpiece of Ladino religious literature is *Me'am Lo'ez* (*From the People Speaking an Alien Language*), 1730–1901, which is an encyclopedia of Jewish knowledge, wisdom, and lore; it was begun by Yaacov Khulli (1689–1732) and after his death, was continued by other writers. Almost every Sephardic home had at least one volume of *Me'am Lo'ez*.

The nineteenth century witnessed a growth of secular literature in Ladino (novels, theater plays, and essays), the appearance of many periodicals, and the emergence of Ladino theater. French influence on cultural life also led to the translation of French novels and plays.

From an artistic point of view the most interesting examples of Ladino literature are folkloric genres—romances, tales, and proverbs. Many scholars collected Judeo-Spanish romances and folklore, which can today be enjoyed at various festivals and on cassettes and CDs.

Today a number of writers such as Matilda Koen-Sarano, Avner Perez, Clarissa Nicoidski, Moshe Shaul, and Asher Amado continue to work in Ladino.

LADINO TODAY

Kol Israel, the Voice of Israel radio station, started broadcasting programs in Ladino in 1948, with the foundation of the State of Israel. In 1979, the Judeo-Spanish team of Kol Israel began publishing a cultural magazine *Aki Yerushalayim*, the world's only magazine published entirely in Judeo-Spanish (in Latin script).

In 1985, a course of Judesmo was offered at Columbia University in New York. Ladino is now being taught in other places in the United States, as well as in France and Israel. Periodicals with pages in Ladino are published in Turkey, Belgium, France, and other countries.

In Spain, there has been growing interest in Judeo-Spanish. Spanish National Radio broadcasts a daily program in Ladino. In recent years many scholarly publications, dictionaries, books, and CDs have been published, and various concerts and festivals of Judeo-Spanish folklore have been organized. There are several Web sites and even chat room sites in Ladino (see list at the end of the book).

It is the author's hope that this book will contribute to the formidable task of preserving and reviving Ladino.

Abbreviations

adj.	adjective
adv.	adverb
Ar.	Arabic
aux.	auxiliary
conj.	conjunction
dim.	diminutive
f.	feminine
Fr.	French
H.	Hebrew
imp.	imperative
ind.	indicative
inf.	infinitive
lit.	literally
m.	masculine
n.	noun
neut.	neuter
obj.	object
p.	person
pl.	plural
prep.	preposition
s.	singular
s.o.	someone
s.th.	something
Sp.	Spanish
subj.	subjunctive
T.	Turkish
v.	verb
var.	variant
Y.	Yiddish

Dialects

There is no universal standard for Ladino. Because Ladino-speaking Jews settled throughout very vast and linguistically diverse areas, many dialects emerged and were maintained. While regional dialects are common to most languages, one is usually singled out to become the norm for the language; the Tuscan dialect for Italian is a prime example. However, because the Judeo-Spanish language was stateless and there was no formal political or centralized linguistic authority to unify it, no norm was established. The Hebrew alphabet has no vowels, which led to inconsistencies in writing and spelling when it was transliterated into Latin (or romanized) script and was another factor that contributed to maintaining dialectal differences. Even though the transliteration of Judeo-Spanish texts from Hebrew into Latin letters began very early, it still presents problems today.

The lack of an accepted standard or formalizing structure presents a challenge to the construction of grammars or dictionaries in the Ladino language. In Ladino publications several different spellings of the same word may be found. In some cases, even gender may vary, though this is less common. Words or expressions common to some dialects may be unfamiliar to or used differently by speakers of other dialects. Even if they sound or look "wrong" to one speaker, however, they may be entirely acceptable to others. Additionally, the wide variety of written versions of the sounds may confuse even an experienced scholar, let alone a beginner. This book will follow the transliteration system used in *Aki Yerushalayim,* and indicate the stress where necessary.

The Alphabet and Pronunciation

A	B	D	E	F	G	H	I	J	K	L
M	N	O	P	R	S	T	U	V	Y	Z

Vowels are pronounced as in Spanish:

a	as in arm	kada
e	as in bed	azer
i	as in receive	akí
o	as in door	todo
u	as in soon	muncho

Vowel combinations, or diphthongs, are pronounced as follows:

ie	as in yes	bien
ue	as in quest	bueno

In this manual vowel reduction, present in some dialects, is not indicated.

These consonants are pronounced as follows:

g	as in girl (or as a gutteral **gh**)	gato
h	similar to hot	hazino
j	like the s in pleasure	ojos
k	as in king	kaza
r	trilled as in the Spanish *rojo*	razón
y	as in Yankee	yo

These letter combinations are pronounced as follows:

ch	as in church	chiko
dj	as in gentle	djénero

gz	as in **ex**am	**egz**akto
ny	as in o**ni**on	espa**ny**ol
sh	as in **sh**ore	di**sh**o

The letters **b, d, f, l, m, n, p, s, t, v**, and **z** are pronounced more or less as they are in English.

STRESS

The accent rules correspond for the most part to those in modern Spanish.

1. If a word ends in a vowel, **n**, **s**, or **sh**, the stress is on the **penultimate** syllable:

   Kaza, bienvenidos, yaman, onde, enkantado, meldando, eskriviendo, kalavasikas

2. If a word ends in a **consonant**, the stress is on the **last** syllable:

   Plazer, espanyol, topar, komunidad, merkar, meldar, portokal, sivdad

3. The stress is indicated with an accent for exceptions to the above rules:

   Avlásh, también, buyrún, akí, fábrika, rázimos, sezón, miérkoles

LISIÓN PRIMERA

LESSON ONE

Getting Acquainted

KONVERSASIÓN

En el aeroporto Ben Gurión.

Reina: Buenas tadres, vozotros sosh Sinyor i Sinyora Amado?

Nissim: Si, sinyora. Muy buenas tadres. Me yamo Nissim.

Ester: I yo me yamo Ester. Komo vos yamásh?

Reina: Me yamo Reina. So vuestra giadera. Bienvenidos a Yerushalayim. Buyrún.

Nissim: Munchas grasias. Enkantado.

Ester: Muncho plazer.

Reina: Avlásh el djudeo-espanyol muy bien.

Nissim: Vos también! De onde sosh?

Reina: So de Saray, ma agora moro en Yerushalayim. I vos de onde sosh?

Ester: Somos de San Francisco, ma mis avuelos son de Kastoria.

Nissim: I mis nonos son de Saloniko.

Reina: Eyos avlan djudeo-espanyol?

Nissim: Lo avlan solo en kaza.

Ester: I mozotros perkuramos de avlar djudeo-espanyol también.

CONVERSATION

At the Ben Gurion Airport in Jerusalem.

Reina: Good afternoon, are you Mr. and Mrs. Amado?

Nissim: Yes, Madam. Good afternoon. My name is Nissim.

Esther: And my name is Esther. What's your name?

Reina: My name is Reina. I am your guide. Welcome to Jerusalem. Welcome.

Nissim: Thank you very much. I'm very pleased to meet you. [Delighted.]

Esther: Nice to meet you. [Great pleasure.]

Reina: You speak Judeo-Spanish very well.

Nissim: So do you! Where are you from?

Reina: I'm from Sarajevo, but now I live in Jerusalem. And where are you from?

Esther: We're from San Francisco, but my grandparents are from Kastoria.

Nissim: And my grandparents are from Thessalonika.

Reina: Do they speak Judeo-Spanish?

Nissim: They speak it only at home.

Esther: And we also try to speak Judeo-Spanish.

Vokabulario / Vocabulary

a	to
aeroporto *(m.)*	airport
agora	now
avlar	to speak, to talk
bien *(adv.)*	well
bueno *(adj.)*	good
de	of, from
de onde = donde	where from
en	in
giadera *(f.)*	guide
i	and
kaza *(f.)*	house
komo?	how?
lo *(obj.)*	it
ma	but
mal	badly
malo	bad
mi/s	my
morar en	to live in, to reside in
muncho/mucho	many *(agrees in number and gender)*
muy	very
no	no, not
nono/avuelo/papu *(m.)*	grandfather
ser	to be *(see Lesson 3 for conjugation)*
si	yes
sinyor (Sr.)	Mr.
sinyora (Sra.)	Mrs.
solo	only
también	also, too
vuestro/a/os/as	your *(formal)*
yamar	to call, to name *(s.o.)*
yamarse	to be named, to call oneself

Proper Names

djudeo-espanyol	Judeo-Spanish, Ladino
Kastoria	Kastoria
Saloniko	Thessalonika
Saray	Sarajevo
Yerushalayim	Jerusalem

Ekspresiones / Expressions

Bienvenidos!	Welcome!
Buenas tadres!*	Good afternoon!
Buenos días!	Good morning!
Buyrún! *(T.)*	Welcome!
en kaza	at home
Enkantado.	Nice to meet you. [*lit.* Delighted.]
Komo vos yamash?	What is your name? *(formal)*
Me yamo Rakel.	My name is Rachel. [*lit.* I call myself Rachel.]
Munchas grasias.	Thank you very much.
Muncho plazer.	Nice to meet you. [*lit.* Very pleased.]
perkurar de + *inf.*	to try to + *inf.*

*Note: in Ladino, the Spanish combination **-rd-** is often changed to **-dr-**.

Gramátika / Grammar

Djénero de nombres sustantivos / Gender of Nouns

Ladino nouns are either feminine or masculine. For human beings, gender corresponds to biological sex; for objects, there is no logic. Feminine nouns usually end in **-a**, masculine nouns end in **-o** or in a **consonant**.

aeroporto *(m.)*	airport
kaza *(f.)*	house

The gender of some words may vary by dialect. These are words ending in an -e or a **consonant** and nouns coming from Greek that end in **-ma/-ta**.

kostumbre *(m. or f.)*	custom, tradition
portokal *(m. or f.)*	orange
poema *(m. or f.)*	poem

Nouns that end in **-ad**, **-ud**, and **-sión** are feminine:

la sivdad *(f.)*	city
la virtud *(f.)*	virtue
la lisión *(f.)*	lesson

Pronombres personales / Personal Pronouns

	Singular		*Plural*	
1st person	**yo**	I	**mozotros** *(m.)*, **mozotras** *(f.)*	we
2nd person	**tu**	you	**vos/vozotros** *(m.)*, **vozotras** *(f.)*	you
3rd person	**el, eya**	he, she	**eyos** *(m.)*, **eyas** *(f.)*	they

The form **tu** is informal and corresponds to *tú* in Spanish and to *thou* in old English. The form **vos** (variants: **vozotros/vozotras**) can be used to address many people or as a polite address to one person. The masculine ending **-os** and feminine ending **-as** of the plural pronouns serve to indicate gender.

As in Spanish, since the endings of the verbs indicate the person and number, personal pronouns are often omitted.

Note: Ladino does not have a special form of polite address used in speaking to one person. (The Spanish form *Ud.* is a contraction from the expression *vuestra merced* and appeared after the Expulsion.)

Conjugation of regular verbs (I conjugation, present tense)

Verbs in Ladino are conjugated, i.e, the endings change depending on person and number. Verbs are divided into three groups depending on the suffix of the infinitive. Verbs with an infinitive in **-ar** belong to the first conjugation. (See Lesson 4, page 51, for second and third conjugations.)

Presente Present tense	**Primera kondjugasión** First conjugation	**Verbos regulares** Regular verbs

avlar (to speak/to talk)

Singular	*Plural*
avlo I speak	**avlamos** we speak
avlas you speak	**avlásh** you *(pl.)* speak
avla he/she/it speaks	**avlan** they speak

As in other Romance languages, Ladino has reflexive verbs, which indicate action directed to the subject. For example, **lavar** means *to wash (something or somebody)* and the reflexive verb **lavarse** means *to wash oneself.*

Kondjugasión de los verbos refleksivos / Conjugation of reflexive verbs

yamar (to call, to name someone)

Singular	*Plural*
yamo I call *(s.o.)*	**yamamos** we call *(s.o.)*
yamas you call *(s.o.)*	**yamásh** you *(pl.)* call *(s.o.)*
yama he/she/it calls *(s.o.)*	**yaman** they call *(s.o.)*

yamarse (to be named, to call oneself)

Singular	*Plural*
me yamo I call myself	**mos yamamos** we call ourselves
te yamas you call yourself	**vos yamásh** you *(pl.)* call yourselves
se yama he/she/it calls herself	**se yaman** they call themselves

Egzersisios / Exercises

A. Yena la forma korrekta del verbo.
Fill in the correct form of the verb.

1. Yo (morar) _____ en Safed.

2. Eya (morar) _____ en Estambol.

3. Onde (morar) _____ tu?

4. Mozotros (avlar) _____ portugez.

5. Vozotros (avlar) _____ inglez?

6. Yo no (avlar) _____ turko.

7. Eyos (morar) _____ en Saloniko.

B. Kondjuga el verbo lavarse.
Conjugate the verb **lavarse** (*to wash oneself*).

_____

_____

_____

C. Responde a las perguntas sigentes.
Answer the following questions.

1. Komo te yamas?   _____

2. Onde moras?   _____

3. Komo se yama tu mamá?   _____

4. Onde mora eya?   _____

5. Komo se yama tu papá?   _____

6. Onde mora el?   _____

LISIÓN SIGUNDA

LESSON TWO

The Family

KONVERSASIÓN

En la kafeterya del muzeo Beit Ha-Tfutsot.

Ester: Oy en el muzeo vide una foto de despozorio semejante a la ke tienen los nonos de Nissim.

Reina: Nissim, kontame sovre vuestros nonos.

Nissim: Se yaman Arón i Mazalta Koen.

Reina: Son djenitores de vuestro padre o vuestra madre?

Nissim: Son de mi madre.

Reina: Donde son vuestros avuelos?

Nissim: Mi avuelo es de Yeni-Bazar i la nona, de Saloniko.

Reina: I los djenitores de vuestro padre?

Nissim: Se yaman Avram i Flora Amado i son de Saloniko también.

Reina: Vuestro padre es el ijiko mas chiko?

Nissim: No, es el bohor. Tiene dos ermanas i kuatro ermanos mas chikos.

Ester: Tienes munchos tíos i tías.

Nissim: Si, muestra famiya es grande. Todos mis tíos tienen munchas kriaturas. Tengo munchos primos i mis nonos tienen munchos inyetos.

Reina: Todos están kazados?

Nissim: Kaji todos.

Reina: Savésh komo se kazan los sefardís tradisionalmente?

Ester: Kontamos, es muy interesante.

Reina: Komo es uzo en todas famiyas djudias, el novio toma konosensia de la novia kon el ayudo de una kazamentera, los parientes kedan de akordo de ashugar i de la dota, i los dos se kazan.

CONVERSATION

In the cafeteria of the Beit Ha-Tfutzot Museum.

Esther: In the museum today I saw an engagement photo similar to the one that Nissim's grandparents have.

Reina: Nissim, tell me about your grandparents.

Nissim: Their names are Aron and Mazalta Koen.

Reina: Are they the parents of your father or your mother?

Nissim: They are my mother's.

Reina: Where are your grandparents from?

Nissim: My grandfather is from Novi Pazar, and my grandmother, from Thessalonika.

Reina: And your father's parents?

Nissim: Their names are Avram and Flora Amado, and they are from Thessalonika, too.

Reina: Is your father the youngest son?

Nissim: No, he's the eldest. He has two younger sisters and four younger brothers.

Esther: You have a lot of aunts and uncles.

Nissim: Yes, our family is large. All my aunts and uncles have many children. I have many first cousins and my grandparents have many grandchildren.

Reina: Are they all married?

Nissim: Nearly all.

Reina: Do you know how the Sephardim traditionally marry?

Esther: Tell us, it's very interesting.

Reina: According to tradition in all Jewish families, the groom gets acquainted with the bride with the help of a matchmaker, the relatives agree on the dowry, and the two marry.

Vokabulario / Vocabulary

akí	here
alguno *(adj.)*	one, some
ambezar	to learn, to study
ashugar *(m.)*	trousseau that a bride prepares for herself (clothing, bed and table linens, etc.)
ayegar	to arrive
ayudo *(m.)*	help
azer	to do
bivir	to live
chiko	little, small
despozorio *(m.)*	engagement
djenitores *(m. pl.)*	parents
djudío/djidió	Jew
dos	two
dota *(f.)*	dowry consisting of money and/or estate
el bohor	the biggest, the eldest son
el mas chiko	the smallest, the youngest
empesar	to begin
ermano *(m.)*/**ermana** *(f.)*	brother/sister
famiya *(f.)*	family
foto *(f.)* *	photo(graph)
grande	big
ijiko *(m.)*	small boy
ijo *(m.)*/**ija** *(f.)*	son/daughter
inyeto *(m.)*/**inyeta** *(f.)*	grandson/granddaughter
interesante	interesting
kafeterya *(f.)*	cafeteria
kaji	nearly
kazado*(m.)*/**kazada** *(f.)*	married
kazamentera *(f.)*	matchmaker
kazarse	to marry
ke?/kualo?	what?
ken?	who?
kon	with
konosensia *(f.)*	acquaintance
kontar	to tell, to relate

kriatura *(f.)*	child
kuatro	four
lavorar	to work
madre *(f.)*	mother
maldar *(m.)*	religious school
marido *(m.)*	husband
mas	more
meldar	to read
mirar	to look
mujer *(f.)*	woman, wife
muzeo *(m.)*	museum
novio *(m.)*/**novia** *(f.)*	fiancé, bridegroom/fiancée, bride
o	or
oy *(m.)*	today
padre *(m.)*	father
pariente *(n./m./f.)*	relative
primo *(m.)*/**prima** *(f.)*	first male cousin/first female cousin
saver	to know
semejante	similar
sinko	five
sovre	about, regarding, concerning
tener	to have
tío *(m.)*/**tía** *(f.)*	uncle/aunt
todo *(adj./m.)*	all, every/everything
topar	to find, come across
tradisionalmente	traditionally
tres	three
un/una	one

*The noun **foto** is an abbreviation of the word **fotografia**, which is why it is feminine: **una foto, la foto**.

PROPER NAMES

Beit Ha-Tfutzot	Museum of the Diaspora in Israel
Yeni-Bazar	Novi Pazar *(city in present-day Serbia)*

EKSPRESIONES / EXPRESSIONS

empesar a + *inf.*	begin to + *inf.*, begin + *gerund*
empesar a lavorar	begin/start working
kazarse kon	to marry [someone], to get married
kedar(se) de akordo/akodro	to agree, come to an agreement
komo es uzo	according to tradition, as is the practice
mas tadre	later
tomar konosensia	to become acquainted
vide	I have seen

GRAMÁTIKA / GRAMMAR

Gender

Plural

Nouns that end in vowels usually form the plural by adding an **-s**:

nono grandfather	**nonos** grandfathers
ija daughter	**ijas** daughters
padre father	**padres** fathers

Nouns that end in consonants form the plural by adding an **-es**:

sivdad city	**sivdades** cities
papel paper	**papeles** papers
amor love	**amores** loves
luz light	**luzes** lights

Note how these rules differ from English by comparing:

train	trains	**tren**	**trenes**
potato	potatoes	**patata**	**patatas**

Note that if **s** is located between two vowels it changes into **z**:

mes   **mezes**

Adjectives agree in gender and number with the nouns they modify and form the plural in the same way as the nouns.

un ombre riko a rich man   **ombres rikos** rich men
una famiya rika a rich family   **famiyas rikas** rich families

Articles

The indefinite article (*a* or *an* in English) has different forms for the masculine and feminine: **un, una**. There are some differences in usage with the English indefinite article. For example, the article is NOT used in nominative sentences stating profession, occupation, etc.

Eya es maestra.   She is [a] teacher.
Tu sos elevo.   You are [a] student.

The definite article (*the* in English) has different forms depending on both gender and number:

Singular	*Plural*
el **nono** the grandfather	*los* **nonos** the grandfathers
la **nona** the grandmother	*las* **nonas** the grandmothers

When the singular masculine definite article follows the prepositions **a** and **de**, it contracts as follows:

a + el = al to the   **de + el = del** from the

Possessive Adjectives

Possessive adjectives (such as *my*, *your*, and *his*) are used to show ownership of something (a noun). For example, in the phrase *my house*, the possessive adjective *my* modifies the noun *house*.

Unlike English, in Ladino possessive adjectives must agree in gender and number with the nouns they modify. Note in the following chart of the Ladino possessive adjectives that there are at least two forms for each adjective—singular and plural—depending on whether the noun modified is singular or plural:

Possessive Adjective	Singular Noun Modified	Plural Noun Modified
my	**mi**	**mis**
your	**tu**	**tus**
his/her	**su**	**sus**
our	**muestro/muestra** *(m./f.)*	**muestros/muestras** *(m./f.)*
your *(formal s./pl.)*	**vuestro/vuestra** *(m./f.)*	**vuestros/vuestras** your *(m./f.)*
their	**su** *(m./f.)*	**sus** *(m./f.)*

In the case of *our* and *your,* there are four forms for each adjective, depending on whether the noun modified is singular or plural, feminine or masculine. For example, *muestra* **kaza** means *our house* (**muestra** is singular and feminine because **kaza** is singular and feminine) but *muestro* **papel** means *our paper* (**muestro** is singular and masculine because **papel** is singular and masculine).

Here are some more examples of possessive adjectives:

mi madre my mother   **mi padre** my father
muestra madre our mother   **vuestro padre** your father
muestras madres our mothers   **vuestros padres** your fathers
mi ija my daughter   **mis ijas** my daughters
vuestro ijo your son   **vuestros ijos** your sons
su nono his/her/their   **sus nonos** his/her/their
    grandfather   grandfathers

Egzersisios / Exercises

A. **Forma el plural de los substantivos i los adjektivos i troka el artíkolo del indefinido al definido.**
Form the plural of the nouns and adjectives and change the indefinite article to the definite.

Enshemplo: un nono viejo   los nonos viejos

1. una mujer kazada   _____
2. un ijo chiko   _____
3. una ija chika   _____
4. una tía rika   _____
5. un tío riko   _____
6. una madre buena   _____
7. una famiya djudía   _____
8. una aksión mala   _____
9. un maldar muevo   _____

B. **Forma el plural de los sustantivos i los pronombres posesivos.**
Form the plural of the nouns and possessive adjectives.

Enshemplo: mi kaza   mis kazas

1. Su famiya   _____
2. Tu ermana   _____
3. Su padre   _____
4. Mi primo   _____
5. Tu tío   _____
6. Muestra nona   _____
7. Vuestro ijo   _____

C. **Forma el singular de los sustantivos i los pronombres posesivos.**
Form the singular of the nouns and possessive adjectives.

Enshemplo: muestros ermanos   muestro ermano

1. Sus primas   _____

2. Vuestras tías   _____

3. Sus nonas   _____

4. Mis ijos   _____

5. Tus ijas   _____

6. Muestras famiyas   _____

D. **Yena la forma korrekta del verbo.**
Fill in the correct form of the verb.

1. Mozotros (bushkar) _____ dokumentos sovre muestros djenitores.

2. Mi tía (lavorar) _____ en un muzeo.

3. Eyos (topar) _____ sus parientes en Israel.

4. Mis primos (meldar) _____ en evreo [Hebrew language] en un maldar.

5. Yo (empesar) _____ a lavorar.

6. Vozotros (ayegar) _____ a Saray.

7. Onde tu (lavorar) _____?

LISIÓN TRESERA

LESSON THREE

What Do You Do?

KONVERSASIÓN

Ke azes? Kuala es tu profesión?

En la sala del otel en Yerushalayim.

Malka: O, Ester! Tu por akí, ke azes?

Ester: Malka, me plaze verte. Mi marido i yo estamos en Israel en vakansa.

Malka: Estás kazada? Ke sorpreza!

Ester: Si, mi marido es Nissim Amado.

Malka: Mazal bueno. Onde lavora el?

Ester: El es médiko. I tu estás kazada?

Malka: Ainda no, mi novio es israelí, está en la armada. Estó akí kon mis djenitores i mi ermano. Eyos vinieron para ver a mi novio. Tu lavoras? Onde?

Ester: Ainda no lavoro, so eleva para ser avokata. I kualo es tu ofisio?

Malka: Estudio en la universidad djudia. So estudiante para ser terdjuman. Me agrada ambezar linguas.

Ester: Linguas son difísiles.

Malka: No estó de akordo.

Ester: I ke aze tu ermano?

Malka: El es moendiz en una fábrika, agora está en vakansa.

Ester: Komo están tus djenitores?

Malka: Están muy bien, grasias. Les agrada estar en Israel i les plaze mi novio.

Ester: Ke bien! Mos renkontraremos todos djuntos por la noche en un restorante.

Malka: Kon plazer.

CONVERSATION

What do you do? What is your profession?

In the lobby of a hotel in Jerusalem.

Malka: Oh, Esther! You're here! What are you doing [here]?

Esther: Malka, I'm happy to see you. My husband and I are in Israel on vacation.

Malka: You're married? What a surprise!

Esther: Yes, my husband is Nissim Amado.

Malka: Congratulations! Where does he work?

Esther: He's a physician. Are you married?

Malka: Not yet, my fiancé is an Israeli, and he's in the army now. I'm here with my parents and my brother. They came to meet [see] my fiancé. Do you work? Where?

Esther: I'm not working yet, I'm studying to be a lawyer. And what do you do?

Malka: I'm studying at Hebrew University. I'm studying to be an interpreter. I like learning languages.

Esther: Languages are difficult.

Malka: I don't agree.

Esther: What does your brother do?

Malka: He's an engineer at a factory, and he's on vacation now.

Esther: How are your parents?

Malka: They're very well, thank you. They like Israel and they like my fiancé.

Esther: How nice! Let's all meet together at a restaurant tonight [at night].

Malka: With pleasure.

VOKABULARIO / VOCABULARY

ainda	yet, still
ambezar	to learn, to study, to teach
armada *(f.)*	army
avokato *(m.)*/**avokata** *(f.)*	lawyer
difísil	difficult
djudío *(m.)*/**djudía** *(f.)*	Jewish
elevo *(m.)*/**eleva** *(f., Fr.)*/	student
estudiante	
fábrika *(f.)*	factory
hakim *(m., Ar.)*	judge
halvadji *(m., T.)*	vendor of sweets
hamal *(m., T.)*	porter, errand boy
hazino/malato	sick, ill
israelí	Israeli
kafedji *(m., T.)*	coffee shop owner
lingua *(f.)*	language, tongue
maestro *(m.)*/**maestra** *(f.)*	teacher
marido *(m.)*	husband
médico *(m.)*/**médica** *(f.)*	medical doctor, physician
merkador *(m.)*	merchant
merkar	to buy
moendiz *(m., T./Ar.)*	engineer
noche *(f.)*	night
ofisio *(m.)*	occupation
otel *(m.)*	hotel
para	for
profesión *(f.)*	profession
profesor *(m.)*/**profesora** *(f.)*	professor
renkontrarse	to meet each other
restorante *(m.)*	restaurant
sala *(f.)*	room
sorpreza *(f.)*	surprise
terdjuman *(m., T.)*	translator
tidjaret *(f., T.)*	trade, commerce
universidad *(f.)*	university
vendedor *(m.)*	vendor

vender	to sell
ver	to see
vinieron *(past of venir)*	they came
zanadji *(m., T.)*/artezano *(m.)*/ esnaf *(m., Ar.)*	craftsman, artisan

Ekspresiones / Expressions

estar bien/mal (hazino/a)	to feel well/sick
estar de akordo (d'akordo)	to agree
estar en vakansa	to be on vacation
Komo estás/estásh?	How are you? *(informal and formal)*
kon plazer	with pleasure

Le agradan sus amigos.	He/she likes his/her/their friends.
	   [*lit.* His/her/their friends please
	   him/her.]

Mazal bueno! *(H. + Sp.)*	Congratulations! Good luck!
me plaze, me agrada	I like ... [*lit.* something pleases me]

Note: The subject of the phrase is not I, but what (or whom) I like.
The verb agrees in person and number with the subject. The object
pronoun indicates who is pleased by the subject.

Me plazen los livros.	I like the books. [*lit.* The books please me.]
Mos agrada el otel.	We like the hotel. [*lit.* The hotel pleases us.]
Te plaze estudiar.	You like to study. [*lit.* To study pleases you.]
todos djuntos	all together
por akí	here
por la noche	at night

GRAMÁTIKA / GRAMMAR

Linking verbs *ser* and *estar*

The linking verbs **ser** and **estar**, both meaning *to be*, correspond to the same verbs in Castilian Spanish, and the difference between the meanings of these verbs is the same as in Spanish.

The verb **ser** *to be* is used to denote:

- a permanent quality of the person or object, such as gender, race, nationality, religion, material, etc.

  Eya es mi ermana.   She is my sister.

- a fundamental quality of the person or object, such as size, color, taste, profession, occupation, etc.

  Alberto es profesor de   Alberto is a math professor.
  matemática.

- origin or possession

  So de Yerushalayim.   I'm from Jerusalem.
  El livro es de Moshé.   The book is Moshe's.

The verb **estar** *to be* is used to denote:

- a temporary quality

  Eya está hazina.   She is sick.

- a changeable situation

  La ventana está avierta.   The window is open.

- location

  Izmir está en Turkía.   Izmir is in Turkey.

The following sentences are good examples of the difference in meaning between the two verbs:

Eya está hazina.   She is sick. *(a temporary situation, she will soon recover)*
Eya es hazina.   She is ill. *(a permanent state of illness)*

ser Present Tense (to be)

Singular	Plural
so (se) I am	**somos (semos)** we are
sos you are	**sosh** you *(pl.)* are
es he/she/it is	**son** they are

estar Present Tense (to be)

Singular	Plural
estó I am	**estamos** we are
estás you are	**estásh** you *(pl.)* are
está he/she/it is	**están** they are

NUMERALES KARDINALES / CARDINAL NUMBERS

uno/una	one
dos	two
tres	three
kuatro	four
sinko	five
sesh	six
siete	seven
ocho	eight
mueve	nine
dies	ten
onze	eleven
dodje	twelve
tredje	thirteen
katorze	fourteen
kinze	fifteen

diisésh	sixteen
diisiete	seventeen
diziocho	eighteen
dizimueve	nineteen
vente	twenty

EGZERSISIOS / EXERCISES

A. **Yena la forma korrekta de los verbos *ser* o *estar*.**
Fill in the correct forms of **ser** or **estar**.

1. Komo _____ tu?

2. _____ (yo) bien, grasias.

3. Onde _____ tu marido?

4. De onde _____ tu marido?

5. Eya _____ mal.

6. Eya _____ buena.

7. Mozotros _____ de akordo.

8. Yo _____ amerikano.

9. Agora yo _____ en Israel.

10. Tu _____ kazada?

11. El _____ padre de mi novio.

12. El _____ malato oy.

13. Mozotros _____ djudíos.

14. _____ una fábrika.

15. El _____ en la fábrika.

B. **Treslada al ladino.**
Translate into Ladino.

1. I like the book.

_____

2. He likes Jerusalem.

   _____

3. You *(s.)* like the museum.

   _____

4. She likes her students.

   _____

5. We like our friends.

   _____

6. You *(pl.)* like Israel.

   _____

7. You *(pl.)* like your grandchildren.

   _____

8. I do not like to study.

   _____

9. He does not like his doctor.

   _____

10. My parents do not like my fiancé.

    _____

C. **Treslada al ladino.**
Translate into Ladino.

1. three brothers   _____
2. one sister   _____
3. twenty relatives   _____
4. six hotels   _____
5. nine friends   _____
6. eighteen students   _____

D. **Responde a las demandas.**
Answer the questions.

   1. Komo estásh oy?

      _____

   2. Estásh kazado?

      _____

   3. Komo se yama tu novia?

      _____

   4. Donde es eya?

      _____

   5. Onde lavora tu ermana?

      _____

   6. Komo está eya?

      _____

LISIÓN KUATRENA

LESSON FOUR

At the Bazaar

Konversasión

Frutas i vedruras.

Malka:	Shalom, Ester i Nissim. La sena ayer estava muy savroza. Ma oy vos kero kombidar a una sena sefaradí.
Nissim:	Ester siempre keria ambezarse a kozer komida nasionala.
Ester:	Si, es verdad. Puedes enseniarme komo azer el gizado sefaradí?
Malka:	Kon plazer. Ma agora devo ir al pazar por merkar komanya.
Ester:	Podemos ayudarte i ver el pazar.
Malka:	Peki, devo merkar vedruras i frutas.

En el pazar.

Ester:	El merkado es muy grande i akí ay tantas kozas!
Nissim:	Mira, este zarzavatchi vende vedruras muy baratas.
Zarzavatchi:	Kualo kerésh merkar?
Malka:	Dos kilos de tomates, un kilo de pipinos i uno de sevoya. También kero dos berendjenas grandes.
Zarzavatchi:	Te plazen estas beredjenas? O preferes akeyas?
Malka:	Prefero akeyas, son muy rikas. Kuanto kostan?
Zarzavatchi:	Mueve shkalim por berendjenas i dodje por tomates, pipinos i sevoyas. Ventiun shkalim, un shekel deskonto, dunke es vente por todo. Meteré la komanya en una chanta?
Nissim:	En dos sakos, por favor.
Ester:	I agora vamos a merkar frutas. Pagaremos mozotros. Akí venden frutas.

CONVERSATION

Fruit and vegetables.

Malka:	Shalom, Esther and Nissim. The dinner yesterday was delicious. But today I want to invite you to a Sephardic dinner.
Nissim:	Esther always wanted to learn how to cook national dishes.
Esther:	Yes, that's true. Can you teach me to make Sephardic stew?
Malka:	With pleasure. But now I have to go to the bazaar to buy ingredients.
Esther:	We can help you and see the bazaar.
Malka:	OK, I have to buy vegetables and fruit.

At the market.

Esther:	The market is very big and there are so many things here!
Nissim:	Look, this greengrocer sells very cheap vegetables.
Greengrocer:	What do you want to buy?
Malka:	Two kilos of tomatoes, one kilo of cucumbers, and one of onions. I also want two big eggplants.
Greengrocer:	Do you like these eggplants? Or do you prefer those?
Malka:	I prefer those, they are very nice. How much do they cost?
Greengrocer:	Nine shekels for the eggplants and twelve for the tomatoes, cucumbers, and onions. Twenty-one shekels, one shekel discount, so twenty for everything. Shall I put the produce in a bag?
Nissim:	In two bags, please.
Esther:	And now let's buy some fruit. We will pay [for it]. Here they sell fruit.

Nissim: Kero sesh portokales, dos razimos de uvas i un
kilo de mansanas.

Ester: También merkaremos un kilo de prunas i un de
kayisís.

Malka: Las chantas estan muy pezgadas. Ayde a kaza a
kozer.

Nissim:	I want six oranges, two bunches of grapes, and one kilo of apples.
Esther:	We're also buying a kilo of plums and a kilo of apricots.
Malka:	The bags are very heavy. Let's go home to cook.

VOKABULARIO / VOCABULARY

akeyas	those
ay	there is, there are
ayde *(T.)*	let's go
ayer	yesterday
barato	cheap
berendjena *(f.)*	eggplant
bever	to drink
bolsa *(f.)*	bag
chanta *(f., T.)*	bag
deskonto *(m.)*	discount
dever	to have to, must
dunke	that is
espesial	special
fruta *(f.)*	fruit
gizado *(m.)*	stew
ir	to go
kalavasika *(f.)*	squash
karo	expensive, costly
kayisí *(m., T.)*	apricot
kerer	to want
kilo/s *(m.)*	kilogram
komanya *(f.)*	supplies, food
kombidar	to invite
komer	to eat
komida *(f.)*	meal, food
kon ti	with you
koza *(f.)*	thing
kozer	to cook
kozido *(m.)*	stew
kuanto kostan?	how much do they cost?
mansana *(f.)*	apple
merkado *(m.)*	market
merkar/komprar	to buy
meter	to put
mushteri *(m./f., A.)*	customer

patatas *(f. pl.)*/**kartof** *(m. s.)*	potatoes, potato
pazar *(m.)*	bazaar
peki *(T. pek iyi)*	OK, very good
pezar	to weigh
pezgado	heavy
pipino *(m.)*	cucumber
poder	to be able to/can
poner	to put
portokal *(m./f.)*	orange
prasas *(f. pl.)*	leek
preferir	to prefer
pruna *(f.)*	plum
razimo *(m.)* **de uvas**	bunch of grapes
rikas	good
sako *(m.)*	bag
savrozo	tasty
sena *(f.)*	dinner
sevoya *(f.)*	onion
shekel *(pl.* **shkalim***)*	shekel *(Israeli currency)*
siempre	always
tanto	so many, much
tomat *(m.)*	tomato
valer	to cost, to be worth
vedrura *(f.)*	vegetable
verdad/verdá *(f.)*	truth
zarzavat *(m., T.)*	vegetable
zerzavatchi *(m./f., T.)*	vegetable seller

GRAMÁTIKA / GRAMMAR

Conjugation of regular verbs (II and III conjugations, present tense)

Verbs with the infinitive ending in **-er** belong to the second conjugation, and those ending in **-ir** belong to the third conjugation. (See Lesson One, page 23, for verbs in first conjugation.)

Presente	**Sigunda kondjugasión**	**Verbos regulares**
Present Tense	Second Conjugation	Regular Verbs

komer (to eat)

Singular	Plural
komo I eat	**komemos** we eat
komes you eat	**komésh** you (pl.) eat
kome he/she/it eats	**komen** they eat

Present	**Tresera kondjugasión**	**Verbos regulares**
Present Tense	Third Conjugation	Regular Verbs

eskrivir (to write)

Singular	Plural
eskrivo I write	**eskrivimos** we write
eskrives you write	**eskrivísh** you (pl.) write
eskrive he/she/it writes	**eskriven** they write

Pronombres demonstrativos / Demonstrative Pronouns

Objects that are close to the speaker are preceded by **este/esta** *this (m. and f. s.)* and **estos/estas** *these (m. and f. pl.)*

To indicate objects that are farther from the speaker we use **akel/akeya** *that (m. and f. s.)*/**akeyos/akeyas** *those (m. and f. pl.)*:

este/estos (this, these)	**akel/akeyos** (that, those)
este portokal *(m. s.)* this orange	**akel portokal** *(m. s.)* that orange
estos portokales *(m. pl.)* these oranges	**akeyos portokales** *(m. pl.)* those oranges
esta berendjena *(f. s.)* this eggplant	**akeya berendjena** *(f. s.)* that eggplant
estas berendjenas *(f. pl.)* these eggplants	**akeyas berendjenas** *(f. pl.)* those eggplants

NUMERALES KARDINALES / CARDINAL NUMBERS

ventiuno	twenty-one
ventidos	twenty-two
ventitres	twenty-three
trenta	thirty
trenta i uno	thirty-one
kuarenta	forty
kuarenta i uno	forty-one
sinkuenta	fifty
sinkuenta i uno	fifty-one
sesenta	sixty
sesenta i uno	sixty-one
setenta	seventy
setenta i uno	seventy-one
ochenta	eighty
ochenta i uno	eighty-one
noventa	ninety
noventa i uno	ninety-one
sien	one hundred
sien i uno	one hundred and one

EGZERSISIOS / EXERCISES

A. **Yena la forma korrekta del verbo.**
   Fill in the correct form of the verb.

1. Eya _____ (komer) mansanas.

2. Yo _____ (meter) las frutas en la chanta.

3. Eyos _____ (kerer) komer.

4. Mozotros _____ (dever) ir al pazar.

5. Vos _____ (komer) kalavasikas?

6. Tu _____ (kerer) ambezar ladino?

7. Yo _____ (eskrivir) en evreo.

8. Malka _____ (meter) las peras en una bolsa.

9. Mozotros _____ (komer) kayisi.

10. Kuanto _____ (valer) los portokales?

11. El zarzavadji _____ (vender) vegetables.

B. Treslada estas frasas al ladino.
Translate the following sentences into Ladino.

1. This apricot is tasty.

   _____

2. That apple is big.

   _____

3. Those plums are good.

   _____

4. I eat this fruit.

   _____

5. This city is big.

   _____

6. Put the products/groceries in these bags.

   _____

7. I always buy food in this market.

   _____

8. I want those tomatoes.

   _____

C. Kondjuga los verbos en el presente.
Conjugate these verbs in the present tense.

preferir   _____

vender   _____

meter   _____

D. **Treslada al ladino.**
Translate into Ladino.

23 plums   _____

45 apples   _____

33 bags   _____

67 apricots   _____

52 oranges   _____

LISIÓN SINKENA

LESSON FIVE

Malka's Kitchen

KONVERSASIÓN

En kaza de Malka.

Nissim: Buenas tadres, Malka!

Malka: Seyásh bien venidos! Pasad adelantre! Ester, Nissim, mi novio Rafo.

Nissim: Muncho plazer.

Rafo: Igualmente. Mazal bueno, Ester i Nissim!

Ester: Grasias. Kero ayudar a Malka i ambezar la gastronomía sefaradí.

Rafo: Aséntate, Nissim, i desha a Ester gizar.

Ester: Malka, komo puedo ayudarte?

Malka: Lava las prasas i kórtalas en pedasos. I yo mundo las safanorias i patatas i las korto en kubos.

Ester: Mira, así está bien?

Malka: Peki. Agora pika la sevoya i fríyela en azeite.

Ester: Me keman los ojos!

Malka: Lávate los ojos i pika sevoya debasho de agua yelada. Agora yo adjusto prasas, safanorias, patatas, tomatada, sumo de limón i sal.

Nissim: El guezmo es komo de la kuzina de mi nona.

Malka: Las prasas están bien blandas. Podemos komer. Ayde a la meza.

Nissim: Muy savroza es la komida!

Ester: Bendichas manos! Munchas grasias!

CONVERSATION

At Malka's house.

Nissim: Good evening, Malka!

Malka: Welcome! Come in! Esther, Nissim, my fiancé Rafo.

Nissim: It's a pleasure to meet you. [Great pleasure.]

Rafo: For me, too. Congratulations, Esther and Nissim!

Esther: Thank you. I want to help Malka and I want to master Sephardic cuisine.

Rafo: Sit down, Nissim, and let Esther cook.

Esther: Malka, how can I help you?

Malka: Wash the leek and cut it in pieces. And I'll peel the carrots and potatoes and cut them into cubes.

Esther: Look, is this OK?

Malka: Good. Now cut the onions and fry them in olive oil.

Esther: My eyes are burning!

Malka: Wash your eyes and cut the onions under cold water. Now I'll mix the leeks, carrots, potatoes, tomato paste, lemon juice, and salt.

Nissim: It smells like my grandmother's kitchen.

Malka: The leeks are tender. We can eat. [Let's go] to the table.

Nissim: The food is very tasty!

Esther: Blessed be the hands [that cooked it]! Thank you very much!

Vokabulario / Vocabulary

adelantre	forward
adjustar	to add, to arrange
agua *(f.)*	water
asentarse	to sit down
ayudar	to help
azeite *(m.)*	olive oil
blando	tender
debasho de	under, below, beneath
deshar	to leave, to let
dulsuras *(f.)*	sweets
freyir	to fry
gastronomía *(f.)*	cuisine
gizar	to cook
guezmo *(m.)*	smell
igualmente	also, too
kemar	to burn
kortar	to cut
kubo *(m.)*	cube
kuzina *(f.)*	kitchen
limón *(m.)*	lemon
meza *(f.)*	table
mundar	to peel
ojo *(m.)*	eye(s)
pasad! *(imp. of* pasar*)*	pass!
pedaso *(m.)*	piece
pikar	to chop
prasa *(f.)*	leek
provar	to try
safanoria *(f.)*	carrot
sal *(m.)*	salt
sumo *(m.)*	juice
tomatada *(f.)*	tomato paste
yelado	cold, frozen

Proper Name

sefar(a)dí   Sephardic

Ekspresiones / Expressions

Bendichas manos!   Blessed be the hands [that cooked it]!
deshar + *inf.*   let (somebody) do something
Seyásh bien venidos!   Welcome! [Be welcome!]

Gramátika / Grammar

Modo imperativo / Imperative Mood

The positive imperative for **tu** (second person singular) of regular verbs is identical to the third person singular of the Present Indicative.

lavar	el/eya lava *(3rd p. s.)*	→	Lava! Wash!
komer	el/eya kome *(3rd p. s.)*	→	Kome! Eat!
bivir	el/eya bive *(3rd p. s.)*	→	Bive! Live!

Reflexive particles correspond to the number and person of the addressee and are placed after the verb.

| Lava! | Wash! |
| Lávate! | Wash *yourself*! |

The following are imperatives of some of the most commonly occurring irregular verbs (**verbos irregulares**):

venir	Ven!	Come!
dezir	Di!	Say
azer	Az!	Make!
poner	Pon!	Put!

(Imperatives are continued in Lesson 12, page 139.)

Preposisiones / Prepositions

The preposition **a** can often be translated as *to*.

It denotes direction:

El va a Madrid. He goes [is going] to Madrid.

It can correspond to the dative case in Latin (that is, the case that indicates the noun to whom something is given):

Meldo un livro a mi inyeta. I am reading a book to my granddaughter.

It is used to indicate an animate direct object, as in Spanish:

Desha a Ester kozer. Let Esther cook.

It is used in constructions and expressions:
ir a + *inf.*   to be going to

The preposition **de** corresponds to *of/from* in English.

El es de Bulgaria. He is from Bulgaria.

Preposisiones de lugar / Prepositions of place

en	in
sovre	on
ensima	above
debasho de	under
delantre de/enfrente de	in front of

Unlike Spanish, the preposition **kon** *with* does not connect with personal pronouns: **kon mi, kon ti, kon si** (compare to the Spanish *conmigo, contigo, consigo*).

Egzersisios / Exercises

A. **Forma el imperativo (en tu) de los verbos sigentes.**
Form the imperative (informal) of the following verbs.

lavar   _____

kantar   _____

venir   _____

meldar   _____

pikar   _____

kortar   _____

vender   _____

eskrivir   _____

komer   _____

dezir   _____

B. **Treslada las frasas sigentes al ladino.**
Translate the following sentences into Ladino.

1. Wash your hands!

    _____

2. Write your name!

    _____

3. Cut the carrots!

    _____

4. Peel the potatoes!

    _____

5. Read this book!

    _____

6. Eat [have some] sweets!

_____

7. Give me the salt!

_____

C. **Treslada las frasas sigentes al ladino.**
Translate the following sentences into Ladino.

1. The book is on the table.

_____

2. The potatoes are in the bag.

_____

3. The bag is under the table.

_____

4. I see a girl.

_____

5. I see two books.

_____

6. Wash this little boy!

_____

7. Wash this cup!

_____

8. Go with me to the market!

_____

9. This man is from Izmir.

_____

LISIÓN SEJENA

LESSON SIX

Talking about the Weather

KONVERSASIÓN

Avlando de tiempo

Malka ke está en Yerushalayim avla por telefono kon Ester ke está en Mueva York.

Malka: Buenas tadres, Ester!

Ester: O, Malka! En Mueva York es madrugada. Komo estás?

Malka: Estó bien, grasias, ma aze muncha kalor. Ke tiempo aze en Mueva York?

Ester: Akí también aze kalor, ma oy el sielo está grizo i enuvlado. Dizen ke por la tadre empesa la luvia.

Malka: La luvia es menester para las guertas i los kampos.

Ester: Si, ma a mí no me plaze la luvia. I oy ay muncho aire. Penso ke empesa una borraska. Komo está el tiempo oy en Yerushalayim?

Malka: Aze seko i kayente—trenta i dos grados de kalor.

Ester: Mozotros uzamos Fahrenheit.

Malka: Deve ser ochenta i sesh.

Ester: Ke kalor! Saves, Nissim agora está en Kanadá. Aí aze frío.

Malka: Aze inyeve en Kanadá?

Ester: En invierno aze inyeve, agora no. Ma agora aí aze bastante frío i ay muncho aire.

Malka: Me plaze la inyeve, raramente la tengo visto.

Ester: Ven a América en invierno i ayde a los montes. Aí ay muncha inyeve.

Malka: Bashustoné! Pensaré en esto. I agora devo terminar.

Ester: Mándale saludos de mi parte a tu novio.

Malka: Grasias, saludos a Nissim. Keda en bonora!

CONVERSATION

Talking about the Weather

Malka, who is in Jerusalem, is speaking on the telephone to Esther in New York.

Malka: Good afternoon, Esther!

Esther: Oh, Malka! In New York it's very early morning [dawn]. How are you?

Malka: I'm fine, thank you, though it's very hot. What is the weather like in New York?

Esther: It's also hot here, but today the sky is gray and cloudy. They say it will start raining in the afternoon.

Malka: The orchards and fields need rain [rain is necessary for the orchards and fields].

Esther: Yes, but I don't like rain. And today it's very windy. I think there's going to be a thunderstorm [a thunderstorm is starting]. What is the weather like today in Jerusalem?

Malka: It's dry and hot—thirty-two degrees Celsius.

Esther: We use Fahrenheit.

Malka: It must be eighty-six.

Esther: So hot! You know, Nissim is now in Canada. It's cold there.

Malka: Does it snow in Canada?

Esther: In winter it snows, but not now. But now it's rather cold and very windy there.

Malka: I like snow; I've rarely [rather rarely] seen it.

Esther: Come to America in winter and let's go to the mountains. There's a lot of snow there.

Malka: With pleasure! I will think about it. And now I have to go.

Esther: Give my best wishes to your fiancé.

Malka: Thanks, greetings to Nissim. Be well!

VOKABULARIO / VOCABULARY

aí	there
aire *(m.)*	air, wind
bashustoné *(T.)*	with pleasure
bastante	enough, quite, rather
borraska *(f.)*	thunderstorm
empesar	to begin
enuvlado	cloudy
enverano *(m.)*	summer
faltar/azer falta	to miss, to lack something
frío *(m.n./adj.)*	cold
grado *(m.)*	degree
grizo	gray
guerta *(f.)*	orchard, garden
invierno *(m.)*	winter
inyeve *(f.)*/**nieve** *(f.)*	snow
kalor *(f.)*	heat
kampo *(m.)*	field
kayente	hot
kuando?	when?
luvia *(f.)*	rain
madrugada *(f.)*	early morning, dawn
menester *(m.)*	necessity, need
monte *(m.)*	mountain
nuve *(f.)*	cloud
otonyo *(m.)*	autumn, fall
para	for
pensar (en)	to think (about)
primavera *(f.)*	spring
raramente	rarely
raya *(f.)*	lightning
seko	dry
sezón *(f.)*	season
sielo *(m.)*	sky
telefono *(m.)*	telephone
temperatura *(f.)*	temperature
terminar	to end, to finish

tiempo *(m.)*	time, weather
uzar	to use

PROPER NAMES

Amérika	America
Kanadá	Canada
Mueva York	New York

EKSPRESIONES / EXPRESSIONS

En ke sezón estamos?	What is the season now? [What season are we in?]
Estamos en primavera.	It's spring. [We're in spring.]
Ke tiempo aze? Komo está el tiempo?	What is the weather like?
Keda en bonora!	Be well!
Mandalde saludos de mi parte a ...	Send [Give] *(formal)* my best wishes [regards] to ...
Mándale saludos de mi parte a ...	[Send] Give *(informal)* my best wishes [regards] to ...

GRAMÁTIKA / GRAMMAR

Impersonal constructions

Ladino often uses impersonal constructions, especially in relation to the weather and events that do not depend on an individual.

Sometimes impersonal verbs such as **inyevar** *to snow* or **luviar** *to rain* are used in the third person singular (as in Spanish).

Oy inyeva.	Today it's snowing.

In Ladino there is more frequent use of forms of the verb **azer** *to do, to make* (compare to *hacer* in Spanish) with a noun. In these cases the verb **azer** is also used in the third person singular.

Aze luvia.	It's raining.
Aze inyeve.	It's snowing.

Azer is also used with the same nouns as in Spanish:

Aze sol. (*Hace sol*)	It's sunny.
Aze frío. (*Hace frío*)	It's cold.

When English uses the construction *there is/there are* in a descriptive phrase, Ladino uses the frozen impersonal form **ay** (of the verb **aver**), which does not change regardless of the number of objects (compare to *hay* in Spanish).

En la sala ay dos ventanas.	There are two windows in the room.
Aí ay muncha inyeve.	There is a lot of snow there.

Quantitative and collective nouns

To designate both *many* and *much* Ladino uses one word, **muncho** (*var.* **mucho**), which agrees in gender with the noun to which it refers:

muncha inyeve	a lot of snow
muncho tiempo	a lot of time

The plural form of the word **muncho** indicates that the noun is quantitative (in that case it corresponds to *many*, or *a lot of* followed by the plural), while the singular form is used with collective nouns (compare with *much*, or *a lot of* followed by the singular), which cannot be used in the plural:

munchos anyos	many years
munchas oras	many hours
muncho kavé	a lot of coffee
muncha karne	a lot of meat

EGZERSISIOS / EXERCISES

A. **Yena la forma korrekta del verbo.**
Fill in the correct form of the verb.

1. Oy _____ (azer) luvia.
2. No _____ (aver) viento.
3. En la klase _____ (aver) munchos elevos.
4. En enverano _____ (azer) muncha kalor.
5. En invierno _____ (azer) frío.
6. En otonyo _____ (aver) munchos aires.

B. **Treslada las frasas sigentes al ladino.**
Translate the following sentences into Ladino.

1. What is the weather like today?

   _____

2. It's cold and windy.

   _____

3. And here it's hot and dry.

   _____

4. It's raining.

   _____

5. It's snowing.

   _____

6. A thunderstorm is coming [beginning].

   _____

7. The sky is gray and cloudy.

   _____

8. It's not raining.

_____

9. I don't like the heat.

_____

C. **Treslada las frasas sigentes al ladino.**
Translate the following sentences into Ladino.

1. There are many rooms [oda/sala] in the house.

_____

2. There's a lot of air in the room.

_____

3. There is a lot of time.

_____

4. What is the season now?

_____

5. It's fall now.

_____

6. It's not hot, the sky is cloudy, and it's raining

_____

7. Send my best wishes to your parents.

_____

D. **Responde a las demandas sigentes.**
Answer the following questions.

1. En ke sezón estamos?

_____

2. Ke tiempo aze oy?

_____

3. Aze frío oy?

_____

4. Aze luvia?

_____

5. Ay aire?

_____

6. Ay nuves?

_____

7. Kuala es la temperatura oy?

_____

8. Kuando aze kalor?

_____

9. Kuando inyeva?

_____

E. **Yena kon la forma korrekta de** *muncho.*
Fill in with the correct forms of **muncho.**

1. _____ portokales

2. _____ mansanas

3. _____ tiempo

4. _____ inyeve

5. _____ chantas

6. _____ pipinos

LISIÓN SETENA

LESSON SEVEN

Jewish Holidays

Konversasión

Fiestas djudías

En kaza de Malka.

Malka:	Vengásh en buen ora! Ke ay de muevo?
Ester:	Vimos una ekspozisión en el Muzeo Beit ha-Tfutsot.
Malka:	Kuala ekspozisión? La última ves kuando fui al muzeo era el anyo pasado.
Nissim:	La ekspozisión dedikada a las fiestas djudías. Es muy interesante.
Ester:	Agora sé la diferensia entre las kostumbres ashkenazís i sefaradís.
Nissim:	Somos todos djudiós i la relijión es la misma, ma komo muestros antepasados bivían en diferentes partes del mundo, las kostumbres ke se formaron son diferentes.
Ester:	Kualo, por enshemplo, komemos los sefardim komo yerva amarga durante el Pesah?
Malka:	Ke demanda! Komemos lechuga, porke es amarga—*maror*.
Nissim:	Si, porke muestros avós bivían en tierras kayentes, onde en avril ya ay lechuga. Los ashkenazim bivían en tierras frías, ayá no ay vedrura freska en avril. Por eso komen rávano en Pesah. La ekspozisión amostra varias fiestas—Rosh ha-Shana, Hanuka, Pesah, Purim, Sukot—komo se selebran en diversas komunidades.
Malka:	Yo sé ke durante Hanuka mozotros azemos birmuelos, i los ashkenazim azen latkes de kartof.
Nissim:	I la tradisión de djugar en *sivón* o *dreidel* vino de los ashkenazim. Los sefardim djugavan kartas.
Ester:	La fiesta ke es muy importante para mozotros i tiene menos importansia para los ashkenazim es Tu Be-Shvat, o komo la yamamos, las Frutas.

CONVERSATION

Jewish Holidays

At Malka's house.

Malka: Welcome! What's new?

Esther: We saw an exhibit at the Museum Beit ha-Tfutsot.

Malka: Which exhibit? The last time I was in the museum was last year.

Nissim: The exhibit about Jewish holidays. It's very interesting.

Esther: Now I know the difference between Ashkenazic and Sephardic traditions.

Nissim: We are all Jews, and the religion is the same, but since our ancestors lived in different parts of the world, different traditions developed [the traditions that developed are different].

Esther: For example, what do we, Sephardim, eat as bitter herbs during Pesach?

Malka: What a question! We eat lettuce because it's bitter—*maror*.

Nissim: Yes, because our ancestors lived in warm countries where there's already lettuce in April. Ashkenazim lived in cold countries where there are no fresh herbs in April. So they eat horseradish for Pesach. The exhibit shows various holidays—Rosh Ha-Shanah, Chanukah, Pesach, Purim, Sukkot—and how they are celebrated in different communities.

Malka: I know that during Chanukah we make *birmuelos* and the Ashkenazim make potato latkes.

Nissim: And the tradition of playing *svivon* or *dreidel* came from the Ashkenazim. The Sephardim played cards.

Esther: A holiday that is very important for us, and that has less importance for the Ashkenazim, is Tu Be-Shvat, or *Frutas*, as we call it.

Malka: I los ashkenazim no la selebran?

Ester: Agora en Israel i en algunos lugares en los Estados
Unidos komensan a selebrar. I mozotros en este día
komemos muncha fruta freska i seka, ke eyos no tenían.

Nissim: De todas fiestas djudías me agrada más Purim. Akel día
siempre me siento komo una kriatura pekenya.

Malka: I a mi me plaze Purim también.

Ester: Peki, prepararemos los vestidos para Purim i
kantaremos koplas de Purim.

Purim, Purim *lanu*,
Pesah en la mano,
Ya vino enverano,
Para ir al kampo.

Malka:	And the Ashkenazim don't celebrate it?
Esther:	Nowadays they are starting to celebrate it in Israel and in some places in the United States. And on that day we eat a lot of fruit, both fresh and dried, that they did not have.
Nissim:	I like Purim most of all Jewish holidays. On that day I always feel like a small child.
Malka:	I also like Purim.
Esther:	Great, let's prepare Purim costumes and sing Purim songs.

Purim, our Purim,
Passover is at hand,
Summer is coming,
Time to go to the country.

VOKABULARIO / VOCABULARY

amargo	bitter
amostrar	to demonstrate, to show
antepasado *(m.)*	ancestor
anyo *(m.)*	year
avós	forebears/ancestors
avril *(m.)*	April
ayá	there
birmuelo *(m.)*	doughnut
bivir	to live
dedikado	dedicated
demanda *(f.)*	question
diferensia *(f.)*	difference
diferente	different
diverso	diverse
djugar	to play
durante	during
ekspozisión *(f.)*	exhibit, exhibition
enshemplo *(m.)*	example
entre	between
enverano *(m.)*	summer
era	was
fiesta *(f.)*	holiday, party
formarse	to be formed, to form itself
fresko	fresh
frio *(adj.)*	cold
fui	I went
interesante	interesting
kampo *(m.)*	field
kantar	to sing
kartas *(f. pl.)*	cards
kayente	warm
komer	to eat
komunidad *(f.)*	community
koplas *(f. pl.)*	songs, ballads
kostumbre *(m./f.)*	tradition, custom, rite
kriatura *(f.)*	child

lechuga *(f.)*	lettuce
legumes *(m. pl.)*	legumes
lugar *(m.)*	place, seat
mano *(f.)*	hand
mizmo	same
mundo *(m.)*	world
muzeo *(m.)*	museum
otro	other, another
parte *(f.)*	part
pasado	past
pekenyo	little, small
porke	because, why
preparar	to prepare
rávano *(m.)*	horseradish
relijión *(f.)*	religion
selebrar	to celebrate
sentirse	to feel [oneself]
siempre	always
tierra *(f.)*	land
todos	all, everybody, everything
tradisión *(f.)*	tradition
último	last
vario	various
vedrura *(f.)*	vegetables
vestido *(m.)*	dress, costume
vimos*	we saw
vino**	he/she/it came
ya	already
yerva *(f.)*	grass, herb

*1st person, plural, past tense of the verb **ver**
3rd person, singular, past tense of the verb **venir

PROPER NAMES

Ashkenazim	Ashkenazi Jews, East-European (Yiddish-speaking) Jews
Hanuka	Jewish holiday

los Estados Unidos	the United States
Pesah	Pesach, Jewish Holiday, Passover
Purim	Jewish holiday, celebrated with a carnival
Rosh ha-Shana	Jewish New Year
Sukot	Jewish holiday, Feast of Tabernacles
Tu Be-Shvat (Frutas)	Jewish holiday

Hebrew and Yiddish words

lanu *(H.)*	our
latkes *(Y.)*	potato pancakes
maror *(H.)*	bitter
svivón *(H.)*/**dreidel** *(Y.)*	spinning top

Días de la semana   Days of the week

alhad *(Ar.)*	Sunday
lunes	Monday
martes	Tuesday
miérkoles	Wednesday
djueves	Thursday
viernes	Friday
shabat	Saturday
semana *(f.)*	week
día *(m.)*	day

Mes/Mezes   Month(s)

enero	January
fevrero	February
marso	March
avril	April
mayo	May
djunio	June
djulio	July
agosto	August
septembre	September
oktobre	October

novembre	November
desembre	December

The word **día, mes,** the names of the days of the week, and names of the months are masculine: **un día, los días, el lunes, el viernes, el fevrero.**

The days of the week and names of the months *are not capitalized.*

EKSPRESIONES / EXPRESSIONS

dos vezes	twice
Ke ay de muevo?	What's new?
los dos/las dos	both
por enshemplo	for example
ser importante/	to be important,
tener importansia	to have importance
una ves	once
Vengásh en buen ora!/Bonora!	Welcome!
ves *(f.)*	time

GRAMÁTIKA / GRAMMAR

Irregular Verbs (Present Tense)

ir (to go)

Singular	Plural
vo I go	**vamos** we go
vas you go	**vash** you *(pl.)* go
va he/she goes	**van** they go

venir (to come)

Singular	Plural
vengo I come	**venimos** we come
vienes you come	**venísh** you *(pl.)* come
viene he/she/it comes	**vienen** they come

tener (to have)

Singular	Plural
tengo I have	**tenemos** we have
tienes you have	**tenésh** you *(pl.)* have
tiene he/she/it has	**tienen** they have

azer (to do, make)

Singular	Plural
ago I do	**azemos** we do
azes you do	**azésh** you *(pl.)* do
aze he/she/it does	**azen** they do

dizer/dezir (to say)

Singular	Plural
digo I say	**dizimos** we say
dizes you say	**dizísh** you *(pl.)* say
dize he/she/it says	**dizen** they say

saver (to know, can)

Singular	Plural
sé I know	**savemos** we know
saves you know	**savésh** you *(pl.)* know
save he/she/it knows	**saven** they know

Constructions a + *infinitive*

Construction **ir a** + *infinitive* denotes the immediate future:

Yo a meldar este livro.	I'm going to read this book.
Eya va a komer birmuelos.	She's going to eat doughnuts.

Construction **empesar a** + *infinitive* denotes the beginning of an action:

Empeso a meldar este livro.	I'm beginning to read this book.
Eya empesa a komer birmuelos.	She's starting to eat doughnuts.

EGZERSISIOS / EXERCISES

A. Yena la forma korrekta del verbo.
Fill in the correct form of the verb.

1. Yo _____ (ir) al pazar.
2. Ke tu _____ (azer)?
3. Yasmin _____ (venir) oy.
4. Yo _____ (venir) del muzeo.
5. Tu _____ (saver) fiestas djudías?
6. Mozotros _____ (ir) al teatro.
7. Pekenyas kriaturas no _____ (saver) meldar.
8. Ke _____ (azer) el?
9. Vos _____ (tener) tiempo?
10. Yo _____ (saver) meldar en ladino.

B. Treslada las frasas sigentes al ladino.
Translate the following sentences into Ladino.

1. I can [know how to] speak Hebrew.

   _____

2. Can you write in Spanish?

   _____

3. What do you *(s.)* say?

   _____

4. I say I'm doing it only today.

   _____

5. She's going to do it today.

   _____

6. We are starting to fry doughnuts.

    _____

7. We're going to fry doughnuts.

    _____

8. They're beginning to celebrate Chanukah.

    _____

9. They're going to celebrate Chanukah.

    _____

10. I'm making a Purim costume.

    _____

11. I'm going to make a costume.

    _____

12. I am starting to make a costume.

    _____

13. She says she is going to help me.

    _____

14. Where are you going?

    _____

15. Where does she come from?

    _____

16. Who is going to come?

    _____

LISIÓN OCHENA

LESSON EIGHT

At a Concert

KONVERSASIÓN 1

En el konserto

En la resepsión del otel en Yerushalayim.

Nissim: Shalom, Malka. Estás livre esta noche?

Malka: Si. A onde kerésh ir?

Ester: Oy ay un konserto de la kantadera Yasmin Levy. Kanta en ladino.

Nissim: Keres ir kon mozotros?

Malka: Klaro, iré kon plazer. Ya tenésh merkado los bilietos?

Ester: Los merkímos ayer.

Nissim: Kompramos un bilieto para ti también i te kombidamos al konserto.

Malka: Munchas grasias.

Antes del konserto.

Ester: Onde están muestros lugares?

Nissim: En la tresera sira de parter, en el sentro.

Ester: Los tengo topado.

Malka: O, ke bueno! Los lugares son buenísimos!

KONVERSASIÓN 2

Después del konserto.

Ester: Me plaze la múzika djudeo-espanyola.

Malka: I a mí también. Me agradan las romansas i las kantigas folklórikas. Una ves mi novio i yo sintimos un konserto de kantadores amatores. Mos plazió muncho. Era un konserto de la kompetisión yamada *Festiladino*.

Ester: Fantástiko! Ken organizó esta kompetisión i onde tuvo lugar?

CONVERSATION 1

At a concert

At the reception desk of a hotel in Jerusalem.

Nissim: Shalom, Malka. Are you free tonight?
Malka: Yes. Where do you want to go?
Esther: Today there's a concert by the singer Yasmin Levy. She sings in Ladino.
Nissim: Do you want to go with us?
Malka: Sure, with pleasure. Did you buy the tickets already?
Esther: Yes, we bought them yesterday.
Nissim: We bought a ticket for you, too, and we're inviting you to the concert.
Malka: Thank you very much.

Before the concert.

Esther: Where are our seats?
Nissim: In the third row of the orchestra, in the center.
Esther: I've found them.
Malka: Oh, how nice! These are the best seats!

CONVERSATION 2

After the concert.

Esther: I like Judeo-Spanish music.
Malka: So do I. I like romances and folk songs. Once my fiancé and I heard a concert of amateur singers. We liked it very much. It was a concert of the competition called *Festiladino*.
Esther: How exciting! Who organized that competition, and where did it take place?

Malka: Tuvo lugar akí, en Yerushalayim, en el kuadro del Festival de Artes de Yerushalayim.

Nissim: Kualas eran las reglas de partisipasión?

Malka: A, las reglas eran muy interesantes. Esta kompetisión era para amostrar ke muestra lingua está biva i para propajar su folklor i kreasión literaria; las poezías i múzika devían ser muevas i orijinales i los kantadores o kantaderas devían ser amatores.

Ester: Penso ke munchos tomaron parte en la kompetisión, ma pokos ayegaron al final.

Malka: Tienes razón. Ma los ke resivieron premios eran muy buenos.

Malka: It took place here in Jerusalem, as part of the Jerusalem Art
           Festival.

Nissim: What were the rules for participating?

Malka: Oh, the rules were very interesting. The competition was to
           demonstrate that our language is still alive and to spread its
           folklore and creative literary work; the verses and music
           had to be new and original, and the singers, amateurs.

Esther: I suppose that many people participated in the competition,
           but few made it to the final.

Malka: You're right. However, those who got the prizes were very
           good.

VOKABULARIO / VOCABULARY

amator *(m.)*	amateur
amostrar	to demonstrate, to show
aparejar	to prepare
arekojer/arrekojer	to collect, to gather
ayer	yesterday
bilieto *(m.)*	ticket
buenisimos	excellent, best
dever	to have to, must/should
fantástiko	terrific, exciting
festival de artes *(m.)*	art festival
final	final
folklor *(m.)*	folklore
folklóriko *(adj.)*	folk
kantadera *(f.)*	singer
kantador *(m.)*	singer
kantiga/kantika *(f.)*	song
kerer	to want
kompetisión *(f.)*	contest, competition
kompozar	to compose
konserto *(m.)*	concert
kreasión *(f.)*	creativity
literario	literary
livre *(adj.)*	free
maraviya *(f.)*	marvel
muevo	new
múzika *(f.)*	music
organizar	to organize
orijinal	original
parte *(f.)*	part
parter *(m.)*	orchestra *(seating section in a theater)*, parterre
partisipasión *(f.)*	participation
poezía *(f.)*	poetry, verses
poko	little, small
premio *(m.)*	prize, award

propajar	to propagate
regla *(f.)*	rule, requirement
resivir	to receive, to get
romansa *(f.)*	romance, ballad
sentir	to listen, to hear
sira *(f.)*	row
toparse kon	to come across *(s.o.)*, run into *(s.o.)*
tuvo*	it took

*3rd person, singular, past of the verb **tener** (see **tener lugar** below)

PROPER NAME

Festival de Artes de Yerushalayim   Jerusalem Arts Festival

EKSPRESIONES / EXPRESSIONS

en el kuadro de	within the context of
(está) klaro	sure
esta noche	tonight
estar bivo	to be alive
estar livre	to be free
Ke interesante!	How interesting!
tener lugar	to take place
tener razón	to be right
tomar parte	to participate, to take part

GRAMÁTIKA / GRAMMAR

System of verbal tenses

In general, Ladino's system of verbal tenses is more or less similar to that of Spanish; there are some differences, however, in formation and usage.

Present Perfect Tense

The **present perfect tense** is used for actions that started in the past and are still continuing (e.g., *He has lived in the U.S. for five years*); for actions that occurred at some unknown time in the past (e.g., *I have already seen that film*); and for actions that occurred in the past but still have an effect now (e.g., *I have lost my glasses*).

In Ladino, the present perfect tense is formed using one of the two auxiliary verbs meaning *to have*, **aver** or **tener**, in the simple present tense, with the past participle of the specific verb.

Auxiliary Verbs Aver and Tener

The following chart contains the conjugation of the auxiliary verbs **aver** and **tener** in the present tense:

Singular	Plural
aver (to have)	
a/ave I have	**amos/avemos** we have
as/aves you have	**ash/avésh** you *(pl.)* have
a/ave he/she/it has	**an/aven** they have
tener (to have)	
tengo I have	**tenemos** we have
tienes you have	**tenésh** you *(pl.)* have
tiene he/she/it has	**tienen** they have

The paradigm of the verb **aver** varies as shown, and some dialects use the verb **tener**. The verbs **tener** and **aver** are often used interchangeably, showing that speakers do not distinguish between them.

The Past Participle

Regular past participles are formed using the suffix **-ado** for first conjugation verbs:

merkar to buy   →   **merkado** *bought*
Yo ave merkado los bilietos.   I have bought tickets.

For second and third conjugation verbs, the suffix is **-ido**:

komer *to eat*	→	**komido** *eaten*	
Ya tienes komido?		Have you already eaten?	

bivir *to live*	→	**bivido** *lived*	

Eyos an bivido en Yerushalayim munchos anyos.
They have lived in Jerusalem many years.

The following are some of the more commonly used **irregular past participles**:

Infinitive		*Past Participle*	
azer	to do, to make	**echo**	done, made
dizer	to say	**dicho**	said
ver	to see	**visto**	seen
avrir	to open	**avierto**	opened

Degrees of comparison

The comparative degree

Adjectives usually form the comparative through the use of the expressions **mas ... de/ke** *more ... than* or **manko/menos ... de/ke** *less ... than*:

Este bilieto es mas barato ke el otro.
This ticket is cheaper than that one.

Roza es mas alta de Mazal.
Roza is taller than Mazal.

Mazal es menos (manko) alta de Roza.
Mazal is shorter (less tall) than Roza.

Estambol es mas viejo ke Saray, Saray es menos viejo de Estambol.
Istanbul is older than Sarajevo, Sarajevo is newer (less old) than Istanbul.

Dulsuras ke aze Malka son mas savrozas de las ke azen en mi kaza.
The sweets that Malka makes are tastier than those made in my house.

When two equal things are being compared, **tan ... komo** (meaning *as ... as*) is used.

El es tan alto komo yo.
He is as tall as I am.

Eya es tan blanka komo la nieve.
She is as white as snow.

The superlative degree

For comparisons of at least three objects the superlative degree may be used. It is formed by adding the definite article to the comparative form.

flako thin	**mas flako** thinner	**el mas flako** the thinnest
	manko flako less thin	**el manko flako** the least thin
godro fat	**mas godro** fatter	**el mas godro** the fattest
	menos godro less fat	**el menos godro** the least fat

Some adjectives form comparatives derived from a different stem:

bueno – mijor– el mijor	good – better – the best
malo/negro – peor – el peor	bad – worse – the worst
grande – mayor – el mayor	big – bigger – the biggest
chiko – minor– el minor	small – smaller – the smallest

The absolute superlative is formed using the suffix **-ísimo**:

bueno – buenísimo	the best
ermozo – ermozísimo	the most beautiful

EGZERSISIOS / EXERCISES

A. **Troka las frazas según el enshemplo.**
Change the sentences, by following the example.

Enshemplo: El es mas godro ke yo.   Yo so menos godro ke él.

1. Esta komida es mas savroza de la otra.

   _____

2. El gizado es mas kayente ke la sopa.

   _____

3. Este livro es menos importante ke el otro.

   _____

4. Mi lugar es mijor ke el tuyo.

   _____

B. **Kondjuga los verbos en el presente perfekto.**
Conjugate the verbs in the present perfect tense.

Meldar un livro, **avrir** una puerta (open a door), **toparse** kon un amigo.

     _____

     _____

     _____

C. **Treslada las frasas sigentes al ladino.**
Translate the following sentences into Ladino.

1. Your son is bigger than mine.

   _____

2. He is taller than my brother.

   _____

3. This museum is smaller than the Metropolitan.

    _____

4. This market is less expensive than the Central Bazaar.

    _____

5. Fruits are sweeter than vegetables.

    _____

6. An apple is as tasty as an apricot.

    _____

7. He is my best student.

    _____

8. My uncle is older than my aunt.

    _____

9. This is the worst day of my life.

    _____

10. She is the best singer I've ever heard.

    _____

11. The new song is more beautiful than the old one.

    _____

12. This seat is better than that one.

    _____

13. She is as fat as he is.

    _____

LISIÓN MUEVENA

LESSON NINE

Romances and Ballads

Konversasión

Romansas i kantigas

En el arkivo nasional de sonido en Yerushalayim.

Nissim:	Shalom!
Arkivista/Yaakov:	Shalom. Me yamo Yaakov. Komo puedo servirvos?
Ester:	Supimos ke en el Arkivo ay una buena koleksión de romansas sefardís i keremos saver si akí ay las romansas ke kantava mi nona.
Yaakov:	Si, tenemos una koleksión importante de folklor sefardí. Ma para topar la romansa ke bushkásh, debésh saver de ke zona djeográfika eran vuestros avós.
Ester:	Mis avuelos eran de Kastoria, ma komo me eksplikó mi nona, la famiya vino aí de Saloniko.
Yaakov:	Esto es la misma rejión para mozotros. Turkía, Gresia, Balkanes pertenesen a la zona orientala del Mediterraneo. Akí tenemos el katálogo de romansas orientales.
Nissim:	Son tantas! Los sefaradim kompozaron munchas romansas.
Ester:	Porké estas kantikas se yaman romansas?
Yaakov:	La palavra "romansa" es de espanyol. Vino de la ekspresión *hablar en romance,* a diferensia del latín. *Romances* eran dialektos populares usados en Espanya. Mas tadre empesaron a yamar así el tipo de kantiga en *romance* ke trata de la edad media, de reyes, kavalieros i prinsesas.

CONVERSATION

Romances and Ballads

In the National Sound Archives in Jerusalem.

Nissim:	Shalom!
Archivist/Yaakov:	Shalom! My name is Yaakov. How can I help you?
Esther:	We found out that the Archives have a good collection of Sephardic romances, and we want to know whether you have the romances that my grandmother sang.
Yaakov:	Yes, we have an important collection of Sephardic folklore. But in order to find the romance you are looking for you have to know what geographic region your grandparents were from.
Esther:	My grandparents were from Kastoria, but as my grandmother explained it to me, the family came [there] from Thessalonika.
Yaakov:	For us it's the same region. Turkey, Greece, and the Balkans belong to the oriental region of the Mediterranean. Here we have the catalog of oriental romances.
Nissim:	There [they] are so many! The Sephardim composed many romances.
Esther:	Why are these songs called *romances*?
Yaakov:	The word "romance" comes [is] from Spanish. It came from the expression *hablar en romance*, to differentiate [it] from Latin. *Romances* were popular dialects spoken in Spain. Later people started calling this kind of song in *Romance* one that was about the Middle Ages, kings, knights, and princesses.

Ester:	I tiene una relasión kon la palavra *romance* ke uzamos oy en linguas modernas?
Yaakov:	Si, porke estas kantigas fueron kantadas por mujeres i a koruto eran sovre temas del amor.
Nissim:	Meldí ke las romansas se dividen en siklos. Ke siklos de romansas ay?
Yaakov:	Ay romansas ke tratan de amores galantes, de mujeres fieles o de adulterio, ay munchas romansas de batalias i kavalería, otro siklo es sovre kristianos prisonieros de moros.
Ester:	I los djudíos las kantan también?
Yaakov:	Siguro, porké no? Tenemos akí varias romansas de este siklo. Ma también ay romansas sovre temas bíblikos.
Nissim:	Es posivle distingir una romansa?
Yaakov:	Son poemas épikos kon mizmo número de sílavas, 16 (diisésh) o 12 (dodje), en kada línea.

Esther:	Does it have any relation to the word *romance* that we use today in modern languages?
Yaakov:	Yes, because those songs were sung by women and they are often about love themes.
Nissim:	I read that romances are divided into cycles. What cycles are there?
Yaakov:	There are romances that speak of chivalric love, of a faithful wife or adultery, there are many romances about battles and chivalry; another cycle is about Christians who became prisoners of the Moors.
Esther:	Do Jews sing them, too?
Yaakov:	Sure, why not? Here we have several romances of this cycle. However, there are also some romances written on Biblical themes.
Nissim:	Is it possible to tell whether a song is a romance?
Yaakov:	They are epic poems with the same number of syllables, 16 or 12, in each line.

VOKABULARIO / VOCABULARY

adulterio *(m.)*	adultery
amor *(m.)*	love
arkivo *(m.)*	archive
avuelos *(m. pl.)*	grandparents
batalia *(f.)*	battle
bíbliko	biblical
bisavós *(m.)*	forefathers, ancestors
bushkar	to search, to look for
de kavalería	chivalric
destakarse	to stand out
dialekto *(m.)*	dialect
distingir	to distinguish, to define
dividir	to divide
djénero *(m.)*	genre
djeográfiko	geographic
egzaktamente	exactly
eksplikar	to explain
épiko *(adj.)*	epic
espanyol	Spanish
fiel	faithful, loyal
forma *(f.)*	form
fuente *(f.)*	source
fueron*	they went/were
galante	gallant
importante	important
inspirar	to inspire
kada	each, every
katálogo *(f.)*	catalog
kavaliero *(m.)*	knight
koleksión *(f.)*	collection
kompozar	to compose
linea *(f.)*	line
moderno	modern
nasional	national
número *(m.)*	number

palavra *(f.)*	word
perteneser	to belong
poder	to be able to, can
poema *(m./f.)*	poem
popular	popular
pos-bíbliko	post-Biblical
prinsesa *(f.)*	princess
prisoniero *(m.)*	prisoner
rejión *(f.)*	region
relasión *(f.)*	relation
rey *(m.)*	king
saver	to know, to know how, to learn
servir	to serve (*to help* in this text)
siglo *(m.)*	century
siklo *(m.)*	cycle
sílava *(f.)*	syllable
sonido *(m.)*	sound
supimos *(from* **saver***)*	we came to know
tanto	so many
tema *(m.)*	theme
tipo *(m.)*	type, kind
trayer/traer	to bring
tredje	thirteen
uzar	to use
verdá/verdad/vedrá *(f.)*	truth
zona *(f.)*	zone, region

*3rd person, plural, past tense of the verb **ir/ser**

Proper Names

Espanya	Spain
kristiano *(m.)*	Christian
Mediterraneo	Mediterranean Sea
moro *(m.)*	Moor
oriental	Oriental

EKSPRESIONES / EXPRESSIONS

a diferensia de *(f.)*	as distinguished from
a koruto	often
edad media *(f.)*	the Middle Ages
ser posivle	to be possible
tener relasión	to be related to
tratar de	to tell about, to deal with

GRAMÁTIKA / GRAMMAR

Pasado semple (pretérito) / Simple Past Tense

The following charts contain the conjugations for the simple past tense for regular verbs:

1st Conjugation
kantar (to sing)

Singular	Plural
kantí I sang	**kantimos** we sang
kantates you sang	**kantatesh** you *(pl.)* sang
kantó he/she/it sang	**kantaron** they sang

2nd Conjugation
komer (to eat)

Singular	Plural
komí I ate	**komimos** we ate
komites you ate	**komitesh** you *(pl.)* ate
komió he/she/it ate	**komieron** they ate

3rd Conjugation
eskrivir (to write)

Singular	Plural
eskriví I wrote	**eskrivimos** we wrote
eskrivites you wrote	**eskrivitesh** you *(pl.)* wrote
eskrivió he/she/it wrote	**eskrivieron** they wrote

Note: regular verbs of the second and third conjugations, **-er** and **-ir** respectively, follow the same pattern.

Some Irregular Verbs in the Simple Past

ir (to go) = ser (to be)

Singular	Plural
fuí I went/was	**fuemos** we went/were
fuetes you went/were	**fuetesh** you *(pl.)* went/were
fue he/she/it went/was	**fueron** they went/were

venir (to come)

Singular	Plural
vine I came	**vinimos** we came
vinites you came	**vinitesh** you *(pl.)* came
vino he/she/it came	**vinieron** they came

azer (to do)

Singular	Plural
ize I did	**izimos** we did
izites you did	**izitesh** you *(pl.)* did
izo he/she/it did	**izieron** they did

dizer/dezir (to say)

Singular	Plural
dishe I said	**dishimos** we said
dishites you said	**dishitesh** you *(pl.)* said
disho he/she/it said	**disheron** they said

kerer (to want)

Singular	Plural
kije I wanted	**kijimos** we wanted
kijites you wanted	**kijitesh** you *(pl.)* wanted
kijo he/she/it wanted	**kijeron** they wanted

The simple past tense denotes action that took place in the past, action that occurred one time, is not continuous, and took place at a time preceding the speaker's statement:

El le eskrivió a papá.	He wrote to [his] father.
Merkí dos livros.	I bought two books.
Roza fue al konserto.	Roza went to a concert.
Merkimos los bilietos ayer.	We bought the tickets yesterday.
Eyos toparon una kantiga	They found an interesting song.
interesante.	
Ke komitesh ayer?	What did you eat yesterday?
Onde fuetes el anyo pasado?	Where did you go last year?

Diminutive suffixes

Diminutive suffixes **-iko** *(m.)* and **-ika** *(f.)* are widely used, not only with nouns, but also with adjectives.

savrozo tasty	**savroziko** very tasty
chiko small	**chikitiko** tiny

Sometimes a word with a suffix takes on a different meaning, for example:

ijo son	**ijiko** boy
ija daughter	**ijika** girl

In other cases the suffix adds an element of affection as well as the diminutive meaning:

viejo old	**viejiko** old man
morena a dark-skinned girl	**morenika** a beautiful dark-skinned girl

Egzersisios / Exercises

A. **Treslada las frases sigentes al ladino.**
Translate the following sentences into Ladino.

1. I washed the leek.

   _____

2. She bought potatoes.

   _____

3. I read a small poem.

   _____

4. We put together a big collection of Sephardic songs.

   _____

5. Did you go to the museum yesterday?

   _____

6. He wanted to listen to Judeo-Spanish music.

   _____

7. My family came from Turkey.

   _____

8. We arrived at [came to] a little house.

   _____

9. A nice dark-skinned girl sang a romance.

   _____

10. The romance was in Ladino.

    _____

B. **Kondjuga los verbos sigentes en el pretérito.**
Conjugate the followng verbs in the simple past tense.

peterneser   _____

dividir   _____

kompozar   _____

C. **Forma los diminutivos.**
Form the diminutives.

1. Chiko   _____
2. Livro   _____
3. Kantiga   _____
4. Kandela   _____
5. Ojo   _____
6. Kafé   _____

D. **Forma la forma positiva.**
Form the noun without the diminutive.

1. Grasiozika   _____
2. Ijika   _____
3. Saludiko   _____
4. Rozika   _____
5. Kuzinika   _____
6. Prasikas   _____
7. Savrozikas   _____

LISIÓN DIEZENA
LESSON TEN
Sephardic Cultural Centers

KONVERSASIÓN

Sentros de la kultura sefardí
Saloniko, Yerushalayim, Saray
Nombres djeográfikos

En el muzeo Beit Ha-Tfutsot.

Reina: Ola, Ester i Nissim! Bienvenidos al muzeo Beit Ha-Tfutsot.

Ester: Buenos días, Reina.

Nissim: Mos plaze ver vos otra ves. Estásh bien?

Reina: Muy bien, grasias. Oy vamos a ver una ekspozisión dedikada a los prinsipales sentros de la kultura sefardí. Kuando muestros bisavuelos fueron ekspulsados de Espanya, munchos fueron al Imperio Otomano.

Ester: Yo lo sé, ma no entiendo komo era posivle ke los muzulmanes akseptaron bien a los djudíos.

Reina: El sultán Bayazid el Sigundo konvidó a los djudíos a su payiz i les dio algunos privilegios, espesialmente en lugares resién konkistados. Así los djudíos ke se fuyeron de Espanya i mas tadre de Portugal ayegaron a los Balkanes. Munchos se remansaron en Saloniko.

Ester: Ke ofisios toparon los sefardís en Saloniko?

Reina: Algunos lavoravan en las minas de plata, ma mayoriya en produksión de tesido.

Nissim: I porké los sefardís no vinieron a Yerushalayim ke era parte del Imperio Otomano?

Reina: Es un yero típiko. No podían venir a Yerushalayim, porke este territorio no pertenesia a los otomanos en akel tiempo. Fue konkistado por turkos solo en 1517, vente sinko anyos mas tadre.

Ester: I kuando empesó a ser turko, algunos djudíos vinieron akí?

Reina: Si, algunos vinieron i se remansaron, otros fueron a Safed onde era una komunidad muy importante.

CONVERSATION

Centers of Sephardic Culture
Thessalonika, Jerusalem, Sarajevo
Geographical names

In the Beit Ha-Tfutsot Museum (Diaspora Museum).

Reina: Hello, Esther and Nissim! Welcome to the Museum of the Diaspora.

Esther: Hello [good day], Reina.

Nissim: We are happy to see you again. How are you?

Reina: I'm very well, thanks. Today we are going to see an exhibit about the main centers of Sephardic culture. When our ancestors were expelled from Spain, many came to the Ottoman Empire.

Esther: I know, but I don't understand how [it was possible that] the Muslims accepted Jews well.

Reina: The Sultan Bayazid the Second invited the Jews to his country and gave them certain privileges, especially in the newly conquered areas. This is how the Jews who were expelled from Spain, and later from Portugal, came to the Balkans. Many stayed in Thessalonika.

Esther: What jobs did the Sephardim find in Thessalonika?

Reina: Some worked in the silver mines, but the majority in the textile industry.

Nissim: And why didn't Jews go to Jerusalem which was part of the Ottoman Empire?

Reina: You're making a common mistake. They could not go to Jerusalem, because at that time the territory did not belong to the Ottomans. It was conquered by the Turks only in 1517, twenty-five years later.

Esther: When it became Turkish, did some Jews come here?

Reina: Yes, some came and settled, and others went to Safed where there was an important community.

Nissim: I komo algunos fueron a Saray?

Reina: Los Balkanes fueron okupados por los turkos en 1463, i munchos djudíos toparon ayí segunda patria. Así fue formada muestra komunidad.

Ester: La istoria es muy interesante.

Nissim: How did some come to Sarajevo?

Reina: The Balkans were occupied by the Turks in 1463, and many Jews found a second homeland there. That's how our community was created [formed].

Esther: The history is very interesting.

VOKABULARIO / VOCABULARY

akseptar	to accept
antigo	ancient
arresevir	to receive
dedikar	to dedicate
desvelopamiento *(m.)*	development
ekspozisión *(f.)*	exhibit
ekspulsar	to expel
entender	to understand
fundar	to found
fuyir	to run away, to flee
istoria *(f.)*	history, story
komersio *(m.)*	commerce
konkistar	to conquer
kultura *(f.)*	culture
lavorar	to work
mayoriya *(f.)*	majority
nesesitar	to need
ofisio *(m.)*	job, office
okupar	to occupy
parte *(f.)*	part
patria *(f.)*	homeland
payiz *(m.)*	country
perteneser	to belong
posivle	possible
prinsipal	main
privilejio *(m.)*	privilege
produksión *(f.)*	production
remansarse	to settle
resién	recent, recently
sala *(f.)*	hall
sentro *(m.)*	center
sultán *(m.)*	sultan
territorio *(m.)*	territory
tesido *(m.)*	fabric
tiempo *(m.)*	time

típiko	typical
vazío	empty, deserted
yero/yerro *(m.)*	error, mistake

PROPER NAMES

los Balkanes	the Balkans
grego	Greek
el Imperio Otomano	the Ottoman Empire
muzulmán	Muslim
Safed	Safed
el sultán Bayazid el Sigundo	Bayazid the Second
turko	Turk/Turkish

EKSPRESIONES / EXPRESSIONS

alguno/a/os/as	some *(agrees in gender and number with the noun it describes)*
antes de muestra era	before the Common (Christian) Era (BCE)
minas de plata	silver mines

GRAMÁTIKA / GRAMMAR

Passive voice

The passive voice is used in Ladino more often than in English. Its formation is similar to the formation of the passive voice in English: the verb **ser** *to be* is used in the required tense with the past participle of the verb.

La sivdad fue fundada.	The city was founded.

The past participle has different forms for masculine and feminine, singular and plural.

Gender and number in past participles

(See Lesson Eight, page 94 for the rules for the formation of Past Participles.)

Like adjectives, past participles when used as attributes (adjectives) or in the passive voice agree in gender and number with the nouns (or pronouns) they modify. The passive voice occurs when the object of an action is made the subject of a sentence.

El livro *(m. s.)* **fue eskrito.**	The book was written.
La kantiga *(f. s.)* **fue eskrita.**	The song was written.
Los livros *(m. pl.)* **fueron eskritos.**	The books were written.
Las kantigas *(f. pl.)* **fueron eskritas.**	The songs were written.

Imperfekto / Imperfect Tense

In English actions that are continuous are expressed with the compound helping verb *to be* when an action begins and continues for a period of time, either in the past or the present. For example: *I was living there/used to live there for ten years.* In Ladino, the imperfect tense is used very often and indicates a continuing action or process in the past.

Akí *bivían* **los gregos.**
The Greeks *were living/used to live* there.

Kuando entró, yo *meldía.*
When he came in, I *was reading.*

It is also used to designate a repeated action in the past:

Eya *salía* **kada día a la mizma ora.**
She *went out/used to go out* every day at the same time.

The following charts contain conjugations of the imperfect tense for regular first, second, and third conjugation verbs:

kantar (to sing)

Singular	Plural
kantava I was singing/ used to sing	**kantávamos** we were singing/ used to sing
kantavas you were singing/ used to sing	**kantavash** you *(pl.)* were singing/ used to sing
kantava he/she/it was singing/ used to sing	**kantavan** they were singing/ used to sing

komer (to eat)

Singular	Plural
komía I was eating/ used to eat	**komíamos** we were eating/ used to eat
komías you were eating/ used to eat	**komíash** you *(pl.)* were eating/ used to eat
komía he/she/it was eating/ used to eat	**komían** they were eating/ used to eat

eskrivir (to write)

Singular	Plura
eskrivía I was eating/ used to eat	**eskrivíamos** we were eating/ used to eat
eskrivías you were eating/ used to eat	**eskriviash** you *(pl.)* were eating/ used to eat
eskrivía he/she/it was eating/ used to eat	**eskrivían** they were eating/ used to eat

Ser *to be* is an irregular verb. The imperfect tense is:

ser (to be)

Singular	Plural
era I was/used to be	**éramos** we were/used to be
eras you were/used to be	**erash** you *(pl.)* were/used to be
era he/she/it was/used to be	**eran** they were/used to be

Egzersisios / Exercises

A. Forma los partisipios de los verbos, akordando de konkor-dansia en djénero i número.

Form past passive participles from the following verbs, observing gender and number agreement.

tierra (konkistar)   _____

egzersisios (eskrivir)   _____

sevoyas (merkar)   _____

djudíos (ekspulsar)   _____

puerta (avrir)   _____

livros (meldar)   _____

B. Treslada las frasas sigentes al ladino.

Translate the following sentences into Ladino.

1. The Jews were expelled from Spain in 1492.

   _____

2. Some of those expelled were well received in Portugal.

   _____

3. Later they were expelled from there, too.

   _____

4. They fled to various regions of the Mediterranean.

   _____

5. Some were well-accepted in the Ottoman Empire.

   _____

6. This city was founded in 1703.

   _____

7. It (the city) was built on recently conquered land and was called St. Petersburg.

_____

_____

C. **Kondjuga los verbos sigentes en el imperfekto.**
Conjugate the following verbs in the imperfect tense.

konkistar _____

ayudar _____

perteneser _____

arresevir _____

D. **Kambia del aktivo al pasivo.**
Change from active to passive.

Enshemplo: El meldó el livro.   El livro fue meldado por él.

1. Eya eskrivió dos egzersisios.

_____

2. Aleksandro el Grande fundó Aleksandria.

_____

3. Bayazid II kombidó a los djudíos.

_____

4. Tu avrites la puerta.

_____

LISIÓN ONZENA

LESSON ELEVEN

Trip to Safed

KONVERSASIÓN

Viaje a Safed
Merkando bilietos i viajando por otobús

En la estasión sentrala de otobús de Yerushalayim.

Nissim:	Shalom, kero merkar dos bilietos a Safed.
Kashera:	De ida i buelta?
Ester:	Es mas barato merkar de ida i buelta?
Kashera:	Será sinko shkalim por persona mas barato.
Nissim:	Peki, estonses keremos dos bilietos de ida i buelta.
Ester:	Kuando partirá el próksimo otobús a Safed?
Kashera:	Agora son las ocho i ventikuatro. El mas próksimo salirá adientro de sesh minutos.
Nissim:	No tenemos tiempo para nada. Kería tomar un kafé.

Ester:	Kuando salirá el otobús sigente?
Kashera:	Un otobús partirá a las mueve, después otro a las mueve i media, i así kada trenta minutos.
Ester:	Bueno! Tenemos tiempo para tomar un kafeziko.
Kashera:	Los bilietos no indikan tiempo de salida, podésh tomar kualkier otobús, tanto de ida komo de buelta, durante tres días.
Nissim:	Perfekto. Kuanto valen los bilietos?
Kashera:	Sien i ventidos shkalim.
Ester:	(A Nissim.) Tu tienes parás?
Nissim:	(A Ester.) No tanto. (A la kashera.) Akseptásh kartas de krédito?
Kashera:	Akseptamos la mayoriya de kartas. No ay problema.
Nissim:	Akí está mi karta.
Kashera:	Muy bien. Sinya la resevida por favor. Akí están vuestros bilietos.

CONVERSATION

Trip to Safed
Buying Tickets and Traveling by Bus

At the central bus station in Jerusalem.

Nissim: Shalom, I want to buy two tickets to Safed.

Cashier: Round trip?

Esther: Is it cheaper to buy a round-trip?

Cashier: It will be five shekels cheaper per person.

Nissim: OK, then we want two round trip tickets.

Esther: When does [will] the next bus to Safed leave?

Cashier: It's 8:24 now. The next [bus] leaves in six minutes.

Nissim: We don't have time for anything. I would like to have a cup of coffee.

Esther: When does [will] the next bus leave?

Cashier: One bus leaves [will leave] at nine, then another at nine-thirty, so that's every thirty minutes.

Esther: Great! We have time for coffee.

Cashier: The tickets don't indicate departure time; you can take any bus to go there or come back over a three-day period.

Nissim: Excellent. How much do the tickets cost?

Cashier: 122 shekels.

Esther: *(To Nissim.)* Do you have the money?

Nissim: *(To Esther.)* I don't have that much. *(To the cashier.)* Do you accept credit cards?

Cashier: We accept most credit cards. No problem.

Nissim: Here is my card.

Cashier: Very good. Please sign the receipt. Here are your tickets.

Ester: Onde tomaremos el otobús?

Kashera: Tornarásh a la derecha i ayí estará un tabló.

Ester: Grasias.

Kashera: Nesiya buena!

Nissim: Kedésh en buen' ora!

Esther:	Where do [will] we get the bus?
Cashier:	You [will] turn to the right, and there's a display board.
Esther:	Thanks.
Cashier:	Have a nice trip!
Nissim:	Stay well!

Vokabulario / Vocabulary

agora	now
akseptar	to accept
amaniana	tomorrow
después	after
estasión *(f.)*	station
estonses/dunke	then
indikar	to indicate, to specify
kafeziko *(dim.)*	coffee
kashera *(f.)*	cashier
kualkier	any
mayoriya *(f.)*	majority
minuto *(m.)*	minute
nada	nothing
otobús *(m.)*	bus
parás *(f. pl.)*	money
partir	to leave
pedrer/perder	to lose
perfekto	perfect, excellent
próksimo	next, nearest
resevida *(f.)*	receipt
salida *(f.)*	departure
salir	to leave, to go out
sigente	next, following
sinyar	to sign
tabló *(m.)*	display board
tornar	to turn
viaje *(m.)*	travel

Ekspresiones / Expressions

a la derecha	to the right
a la eskierda (sierda)	to the left
adientro de	in *(concerning time)*

bilieto de ida i buelta	round-trip ticket
karta de krédito	credit card
Kedésh en buena ora!/	Be well!
Bonora!/Buen'ora!	
Nesiya buena! *(H.)*	Have a nice trip!
no ay problema	(there's) no problem
por persona	per person
tanto .../komo ...	both ...
tener ambre	to be hungry
tener sed	to be thirsty
tener tiempo	to have time
tomar otobús	to take a bus
tomar un kafé	to have a cup of coffee

GRAMÁTIKA / GRAMMAR

Future tense

The future tense is formed by adding endings to the infinitive; the endings are the same for all conjugations.

kantar (to sing)	**komer** (to eat)	**eskrivir** (to write)
kantaré I will sing	**komeré** I will eat	**eskriviré** I will write
kantarás you will sing	**komerás** you will eat	**eskrivirás** you will write
kantará he/she/it will sing	**komerá** he/she/it will eat	**eskrivirá** he/she/it will write
kantaremos we will sing	**komeremos** we will eat	**eskriviremos** we will write
kantarésh you *(pl.)* will sing	**komerésh** you *(pl.)* will eat	**eskrivirésh** you *(pl.)* will write
kantarán they will sing	**komerán** they will eat	**eskrivirán** they will write

Future action can also be rendered by a form of the verb **ir** followed by the preposition **a** + *the infinitive* (*to be going to do, about to do something*). (See Lesson Seven, page 84.)

Vo a eskrivir.	**Eskriviré.**
I am going to write.	I will write.
Vas a kantar.	**Kantarás.**
You are going to sing.	You will sing.
Va a komer.	**Komerá.**
He is going to eat.	He will eat.
Vamos a meldar.	**Meldaremos.**
We are going to read.	We will read.
Vash a tomar . . .	**Tomarésh . . .**
You are going to take . . .	You will take . . .
Van a ver.	**Verán.**
They are going to see.	They will see.

EGZERSISIOS / EXERCISES

A. **Troka los verbos del pasado al futuro.**
   Change the verbs from past tense to future tense.

1. El fue a Yerushalayim.

   _____

2. Mozotros meldimos en ladino.

   _____

3. Vine de Saray a Saloniko.

   _____

4. Kuando komites?

   _____

5. Komo te akseptaron ayí?

_____

6. Vos sinyatesh la resevida.

_____

7. Eya kantó en evreo.

_____

B. **Treslada las frasas sigentes al ladino.**
   Translate the following sentences into Ladino.

1. We will return tomorrow.

_____

2. She will come back in two hours.

_____

3. Then you will turn left.

_____

4. They will come at five.

_____

5. Will you *(formal)* sing in Ladino?

_____

6. Tomorrow we will go to the museum.

_____

7. After that I will write a letter.

_____

C. **Kondjuga los verbos sigentes en el futuro.**
   Conjugate the followng verbs in the future tense.

sinyar   _____

perder   _____

partir   _____

merkar   _____

ir   _____

ser   _____

LISIÓN DODJENA

LESSON TWELVE

Customs and Traditions

KONVERSASIÓN 1

Kostumbres i tradisiones
Proverbios i refranes

En kaza de Reina en Yerushalayim.

Ester: Reina, vozotros uzásh munchos proverbios i refranes. Mos ambezamos muncho de vos.

Nissim: No puedésh eksplikarmos algunos refranes sefaradís?

Reina: Kon plazer. Mozotros dizimos "Refrán mentirozo no ay." Kualos refranes kerésh ke eksplike?

Ester: Mi nona dizía "Trokar kazal, trokar mazal." Ke signifika esto?

Reina: Esto signifika, en muevo lugar toparás muevo mazal.

Nissim: I porke de los ke tienen suerte dizen ke son nasidos viernes?

Reina: Pensavan ke era bueno naser viernes i ke ken es nasido viernes tiene mazal.

Nissim: I yo me akodro este proverbio, "Yo sinyor, tu sinyor, ken va a dezir *isa* al hamor?"

Reina: Es un treslado del refrán árabo.

KONVERSASIÓN 2

Ester, Nissim i Reina kontinuan su konversasión sovre proverbios en ladino.

Ester: Mi nono dizía,

Tu ijo asta la edad de sinko anyos es tu amo,
a la edad de diez anyos es tu esklavo,
a la edad de diez i sesh anyos es tu konsejero,
de diez i sesh i endelantre es tu amigo o tu inimigo.

Conversation 1

Customs and Traditions
Proverbs and Sayings

At Reina's house in Jerusalem.

Esther: Reina, you use many proverbs and sayings. We learned a lot from you.

Nissim: Couldn't [won't] you explain some Sephardic proverbs to us?

Reina: With pleasure. We say, "There are no false proverbs." Which proverbs do you want me to explain?

Esther: My grandmother used to say, "Change your village, change your luck." What does that mean?

Reina: It means that in a new place you'll find a new fate.

Esther: And why do they say about those who are lucky [have good fortune] that they were born on Friday?

Reina: They [People] thought it was good to be born on Friday, and that a person who was born on Friday was lucky.

Nissim: And I remember this proverb, "I am the boss, you are the boss, who will say *giddyup!* to the donkey?"

Reina: It is a translation of an Arabic proverb.

Conversation 2

Esther, Nissim and Reina continue their conversation about proverbs.

Esther: My grandfather used to say,

Until he's 5 years old your son is your boss,
When he reaches the age of ten, he's your slave,
When he's sixteen, he's your advisor,
From sixteen on, he's either your friend or your enemy.

Reina: Es un proverbio muy konosido.

Ester: Kuando era chika, mi nona dizía "Novia ke la veamos."

Nissim: Eso yo me akordo también, ma me dizían "novio."

Reina: Novio o novia, depende de si es ijiko o ijika. Se dize
          komo bendisión de la kriatura. En jeneral, ay munchos
          proverbios sovre las bodas, komo por enshemplo,
          "Ashugar i kontado te do yo, mazal i ventura te dé
          el Dio."

Ester: Yo sé este, "A la boda sin kombidar no dan lugar."

Reina: Si, era muy importante kombidar a los parientes,
          vizinos i amigos. Para despozorios i bodas azían listas
          de nombres para kombidar. La famiya de la novia
          aparava el ashugar, los musafires lo apresiavan.

Nissim: Muestros uzos i kostumbres eran muy interesantes.
          Kale preservar al meno algunos.

Reina: It's a very well-known proverb.

Esther: When I was little, my grandmother used to say about me, "May we [Let's] see her as a bride."

Nissim: I remember it, too, but to me they said, "groom."

Reina: Groom or bride, it depends on whether it's a boy or a girl. They say it as a blessing for a child. In general, there are many proverbs concerning weddings, as, for example, "I give you a dowry and money, may God give you happiness and luck."

Esther: I know this one: "Without an invitation, there's no place at the wedding."

Reina: Yes, it was very important to invite relatives, neighbors, and friends. For engagements and weddings they made lists with the names of those to be invited. The family of the bride displayed the dowry, [and] the guests admired it.

Nissim: Our customs and traditions were very interesting. We should [there's a need to] keep at least some of them.

VOKABULARIO / VOCABULARY

akonsejar	to advise
akordarse/akodrarse	to remember
amigo *(m.)*	friend
amo *(m.)*	boss, owner
aparar	to display the bride's trousseau *(so relatives and friends can admire it)*
aprender	to learn
apresiar	to appreciate
árabo	Arab
bendisión *(f.)*	benediction
boda *(f.)*	wedding
dar	to give
depender de	depend on, depend upon
Dio *(m.)*	God
djente *(f.)*	people
edad *(f.)*	age
eksplikar	to explain
endelantre	further on
ensenyar/enseniar	to teach
esklavo *(m.)*	slave
hamor *(m.)*	donkey
inimigo *(m.)*	enemy
isa!	giddyup! *(to an animal)*
kazal *(m.)*	village
kon	with
konosido *(m.)*	known
konsejero *(m.)*	adviser
kontado *(m.)*	cash
kostumbre *(m./f.)*	custom
lista *(f.)*	list
mazal *(m.)*	luck
mentirozo	false
mudar	to change place/clothes, to move
musafir *(m.)*	guest
naser	to be born

nasido	born
nombre *(m.)*	name
pariente *(m.)*	relative *(not a parent)*
pensar en	to think about
preservar	to keep, to preserve
proverbio/refrán *(m.)*	proverb, saying
signifikar	to mean
treslado *(m.)*	translation
trokar	to change
uzo *(m.)*	custom
veamos *(imp. of* ver*)*	let's see
ventura *(f.)*	luck
vizino *(m.)*	neighbor

Ekspresiones / Expressions

al meno	at least
en jeneral	in general, usually
kale + *inf.*	it is necessary to
kere dezir	wants to say, means
tener razón	to be right
tener suerte	to have good luck

Gramátika / Grammar

Modo imperativo / Imperative Mood

(continued from Lesson 5, page 61)

Ladino has additional ways of expressing commands aside from the special imperative forms described in Lesson 5. A specific Ladino feature is the usage of a gerund as a second person plural imperative. It is particularly typical of the Thessalonika dialect.

The gerund is a special, invariable form of the verb which always ends in **-ndo**, for example, **hablando, komiendo, viniendo**. To form the gerund, remove the infinitive ending (**-ar, -er, -ir**) of the verb and add **-ando** for **-ar** verbs and **-iendo** for **-er** and **-ir** verbs.

Lili, Nina, viniendo presto akí!
Lili, Nina, come here quickly!

Komo vos plaze, faziendo.*
Do as you like.

*In Thessalonika the "**f**" is retained, as in Portuguese. In other dialects, it has disappeared, as in Spanish.

Negative Imperative

The negative imperative is formed by placing **no** before the second person singular and plural subjunctive forms of the verb. To form the subjunctive **tu** and **vozotros** forms for regular **-ar** verbs, **-es** and **-ésh** are added to the stem of the verb. For both regular **-er** and **-ir** verbs, **-as** and **-ásh** are added to the verb stems.

The following chart shows you how to form the negative imperative for regular verbs in all three conjugations*:

	-ar verb	-er verb	-ir verb
	kantar (to sing)	**komer** (to eat)	**eskrivir** (to write)
tu *(s.)* you	**No kant*es*!** Do not sing!	**No kom*as*!** Do not eat!	**No eskriv*as*!** Do not write!
vozotros *(pl./* *formal s.)* you	**No kant*ésh*!** Do not sing!	**No kom*ásh*!** Do not eat!	**No eskriv*ásh*!** Do not write!

*(For full conjugation of the present subjunctive in all persons for regular verbs, see Appendix I on pp. 179–180.)

To form the negative imperative for irregular verbs, the same subjunctive endings for **tu** and **vozotros** are added to the verb stems. However, irregular verbs have irregular stems. Irregular verbs usually use the first person singular of the present tense to form the stem for the subjunctive. Simply drop the first person present-tense ending and add the subjunctive endings for the **tu** and **vozotros** forms*:

Irregular *Verb*	*1st P. Present* *Tense*	*Stem + Subj.* *Endings* *(tu & vozotros)*	*Subjunctive*
estar to be	**yo estó** I am	**est + és****/ésh**	**estés/estésh**
tener to have	**yo tengo** I have	**teng + as/ásh**	**tengas/tengásh**
venir to come	**yo vengo** I come	**veng + as/ásh**	**vengas/vengásh**

*(For full conjugation of the present subjunctive in all persons for several common irregular verbs, see Appendix III on pp. 182–185).
(Estar has an irregular **tu subjunctive ending.)

Some irregular verbs have special subjunctive stems not derived from the first person present tense:

Irregular Verb	*1st P. Subj.*	*Neg. Imperative*
ser to be	**sea**	**No seas/No seásh!** Don't be!
saver to know	**sepa**	**No sepas/No sepásh!** Don't know!
ir to go	**vaiga**	**No vaigas/No vaigásh!** Don't go!

The following sentences contain negative imperatives of a few useful irregular verbs:

venir to come	**No vengas!**	Don't come!
poner to put	**No pongas el livro akí!**	Do not put the book here!
ser to be	**No seas tonto!**	Don't be stupid!
ir to go	**No vaigas!**	Don't go!

In addition to its use in the negative imperative, the subjunctive mood has many other functions. It is most often used in subordinate clauses that follow main clauses containing verbs expressing desire, doubt, hope or emotion. We'll touch on a few of these functions in the next chapter.

EGZERSISIOS / EXERCISES

A. **Yena kon la forma korrekta del verbo.**
Fill in the correct form of the verb.

1. (Tu dezir) _____ me la vedrá!

2. Kero ke eya (kantar) _____ esta kantika.

3. El kere ke (mozotros aprender) _____ uzos sefardís.

4. Mamá dize a los ijikos ke no (venir) _____ tadre.

5. Dudamos ke el otobús (venir) _____ a tempo.

B. **Treslada las frasas sigentes al ladino.**
Translate the following sentences into Ladino.

1. Do not write! **(tu)**

   _____

2. Do not write! **(vos)**

   _____

3. Do not eat! **(vos)**

   _____

4. Do not come! **(tu)**

   _____

5. Write! **(tu)**

   _____

6. Eat! **(vos)**

   _____

7. Open your book! **(tu)**

   _____

8. Do not open your book! **(tu)**

   _____

C. **Treslada las frasas sigentes al ladino.**
Translate the following sentences into Ladino.

1. Do not be stupid! (**bovo, tonto**)

   _____

2. (*You pl.*) Do not sing this song!

   _____

3. (*You s.*) Come on time!

   _____

4. (*You s.*) Learn the proverb!

   _____

5. (*You pl./formal s.*) Speak Ladino!

   _____

6. (*You pl./formal s.*) Don't speak Turkish!

   _____

LISIÓN TREZENA

LESSON THIRTEEN

At the Airport—Saying Good-bye

Konversasión 1

En el aeroporto
Diziendo adío

Nissim:	Otra ves estamos en el aeroporto.
Reina:	Akí podésh rejistrar los bilietos i bagaje.
Empleado:	Shalom. Ande vash?
Ester:	A Los Angeles. Akí tenésh muestros bilietos.
Empleado:	Grasias. Kale también pasaportos. Sosh amerikanos? Kuantas personas viajan?
Reina:	Solo dos, son amerikanos, si, sinyor. Yo los estó akompanyando.
Nissim:	Por favor, sinyor, akí están los pasaportos.
Empleado:	Muy bien. Kuantas validjas vash a rejistrar?
Ester:	Dos validjas. Podemos también tomar una chanta en el avión?
Empleado:	Peki, no ay problema. Vozotros mizmos avésh arrekojido las validjas?
Nissim:	Klaro, yo mizmo lo ize.
Empleado:	Akí tenésh vuestros dokumentos para embarkar, salida número 5. Buen viaje!
Ester:	Grasias, sinyor. Onde podemos tomar un kafeziko?

Konversasión 2

En un bar del aeroporto.

Nissim:	Ke bien! A la derecha ay un bar, aí ay kafé. Vamos a tomar un kafeziko! Ayde, Reina, eskojad ke vos plaze!
Reina:	Yo kijera un kafé turko i un pedasiko de baklavá.
Ester:	Kerida Reina, avésh echo muestra vijita a Israel un verdadero plazer. I tenemos ambezado muncho.

CONVERSATION 1

At the Airport
Saying Good-bye

Nissim: We're at the airport once again.

Reina: You can check in [with] your tickets and luggage here.

Clerk: Shalom. Where are you flying to?

Esther: To Los Angeles. Here are our tickets.

Clerk: Thanks. I also need your passports. You're Americans? How many people are flying?

Reina: Only two, they're Americans, yes, Sir. I'm seeing them off.

Nissim: Please, Sir, here are the passports.

Clerk: Very good. How many bags are you going to check in?

Esther: Two suitcases. May we take a bag onto the plane?

Clerk: OK, no problem. Did you pack your suitcases yourselves?

Nissim: Sure, I did it myself.

Clerk: Here are your documents for boarding, Gate #5. Have a safe journey!

Esther: Thank you, Sir. Where can we have a coffee?

CONVERSATION 2

In a bar in the airport.

Nissim: How nice! To the right there's a bar, where they have coffee. Let's have a coffee. Go ahead, Reina, choose what you like.

Reina: I would like a Turkish coffee and a piece of baklava.

Esther: Dear Reina, you have made our visit to Israel a real pleasure. And we've learned a lot.

Nissim:	No savemos komo agradeservos. Sosh komo una amiga de munchos anyos, o komo parte de famiya para nos.
Reina:	Para mi estos días también eran muy agradavles. Komo si me uviera topado kon parientes.
Nissim:	Vos konvidamos a muestra kaza en Amérika. Estamos siguros ke muestros padres también estarán kontentos de konoservos.
Ester:	Komo dize mi nona, "muestra kaza es vuestra kaza."
Reina:	Munchas grasias. Espero ke pishin mos veamos de muevo.
Nissim:	Ya están anunsiando muestro vuelo. Grasias por todo, Reina.
Ester:	Grasias, Reina. Un beziko.
Reina:	Adío. Kolay i liviano.

Nissim: We don't know how to thank you. For us, you're like a friend of many years, or a part of the family.

Reina: These days were also very pleasant for me. It's like meeting relatives.

Nissim: We invite you to our house in America. We're sure that our parents will also be happy to meet you.

Esther: As my grandmother says, "Our house is your house."

Reina: Thank you very much. Hope to see you soon once again.

Nissim: They're announcing our flight. Thank you for everything, Reina.

Esther: Thank you, Reina. [Let me] kiss you.

Reina: Good-bye! Good luck! [May it go easily and lightly for you.]

VOKABULARIO / VOCABULARY

agradavle	pleasant
agradeser	to thank
akompaniar/akompanyar	to accompany
anunsiar	to announce
avión *(m.)*	airplane
bagaje *(m.)*	luggage
baklavá *(f.)*	baklava, Turkish sweetmeat
bezo *(m.)*	kiss
dokumento *(m.)*	document
embarkar	to embark
esperar	to hope
kerido	dear
número *(m.)*	number
pasaporto *(m.)*	passport
persona *(f.)*	person
pishin	soon
rejistrar	to register
siguridad *(f.)*	security
validja *(f.)*	suitcase
verdadero	true
viajar	to travel
vuelo *(m.)*	flight

EKSPRESIONES / EXPRESSIONS

a la derecha	to the right
a la eskierda	to the left
adío	farewell, good-bye
ande, a onde	where to
de muevo	once more
estar kontento	to be happy *(shows emotion and requires subjunctive)*
estar siguro	to be sure *(when positive, requires indicative; when negative, subjunctive)*

| **kolay i liviano** | an expression wishing luck for a difficult task; an equivalent could be "Break a leg." [*lit.* May it go easily and lightly for you.] |
| **otra ves** | once again |

GRAMÁTIKA / GRAMMAR

More Uses for the Subjunctive Mood

In the last chapter, we learned that the subjunctive is used to form the negative imperative. The subjunctive also has many other functions.

Presente de subjuntivo / Present Subjunctive

	-ar kantar (to sing)	-er komer (to eat)	-ir eskrivir (to write)
yo	kante	koma	eskriva
tu	kantes	komas	eskrivas
el, eya	kante	koma	eskriva
mozotros/mozotras	kantemos	komamos	eskrivamos
vos, vosotros/vozotras	kantésh	komásh	eskrivásh
eyos, eyas	kanten	koman	eskrivan

The subjunctive is not a tense; rather, it is a mood. *Tense* refers to *when* an action takes place (past, present, future), while *mood* merely reflects *how* the speaker feels about the action.

| **Kero ke venga.** | I want him to come. [*lit.* I want that he comes.] |

In the above sentence, **venga,** the verb in the second or subordinate clause, is in the subjunctive because the verb in the main clause, **kero,** expresses a desire—*I want*. The subjunctive is used in subordinate clauses when the verb in the main clause expresses desire, doubt, hope, uncertainty, or other emotions.

Dudar *to doubt* requires the subjunctive in the subordinate clause because **dudar** expresses uncertainty.

Dudo ke el chiko lo sepa.   I doubt that the boy knows it.

Note that **sepa** is third person present subjunctive of **saver**.

However, when negated, **no dudar** does not require the subjunctive in the second clause, as there is no longer any uncertainty in the statement.

No dudo ke él lo save.   I have no doubt that he knows it.

In the above sentence, **save** is in the present tense indicative mood (the indicative being the mood for declaring an unqualified statement) of **saver**, rather than the present subjunctive.

Kreer *to believe* requires the subjunctive in the subordinate clause when the verbal construction is negative, because there is doubt and uncertainty in saying **no kreer**.

No kreo ke el ijiko sepa tanto.
I don't believe that the boy knows [*lit.* may know] so much.

But when **kreer** is positive, the subjunctive is not used because the statement now expresses certainty.

Kreo ke él lo save.   I believe that he knows it.

EGZERSISIOS / EXERCISES

A. **Yena la forma korrekta del verbo.**
   Fill in the blanks with the correct form of the verb.

   1. Ayer él (merkar) _____ una validja.
   2. Yo no (tener) _____ bilietos a Safed.

3. Mas tadre (merkar yo) _____este livro.

4. Estó kontenta ke mos (ver) _____ otra ves.

5. No dudo ke eya (estar) _____ en Saray.

6. Estamos siguros ke muestra lingua (bivir) _____.

B. **Treslada las frasas sigentes al ladino.**
Translate the following sentences into Ladino.

1. I'm going to Paris.

   _____

2. Here are my ticket and passport.

   _____

3. Where can we check in our luggage?

   _____

4. I have a suitcase and a bag.

   _____

5. Where is Exit #12?

   _____

6. What flight are they announcing?

   _____

7. Are you sure it's there?

   _____

8. She is happy to see you.

   _____

9. He has learned a lot during these days.

   _____

10. We are happy to see you once again.

   _____

11. I am thirsty, she is hungry.

_____

12. To the right there's a new museum.

_____

13. To the left there's a restaurant.

_____

C. **Kondjuga en el presente del subjuntivo.**
Conjugate in the present subjunctive.

poner   _____

azer   _____

saver   _____

venir   _____

D. **Treslada las frasas sigentes al ladino.**
Translate the following sentences into Ladino.

1. I doubt that the weather is nice.

_____

2. She doesn't doubt that the book is interesting.

_____

3. I want you (**tu**) to come on time.

_____

4. My grandfather wants me to learn some proverbs.

_____

5. They don't believe that we speak Ladino.

_____

6. You believe that she sings very well.

_____

Yave de los egzersisios
Exercise Keys

Lesson 1

A. 1. moro; 2. mora; 3. moras; 4. avlamos; 5. avlásh; 6. avlo; 7. moran

B. me lavo, te lavas, se lava, mos lavamos, vos lavásh, se lavan

Lesson 2

A. 1. las mujeres kazadas; 2. los ijos chikos; 3. las ijas chikas; 4. las tías rikas; 5. los tíos rikos; 6. las madres buenas; 7. las famiyas djudías; 8. las aksiones malas; 9. los maldares muevos

B. 1. sus famiyas; 2. tus ermanas; 3. sus djenitores; 4. mis primos; 5. tus tíos; 6. muestras nonas; 7. vuestros ijos

C. 1. su prima; 2. vuestra tía; 3. su nona; 4. mi ijo; 5. tu ija 6. muestra famiya

D. 1. bushkamos; 2. lavora; 3. topan; 4. meldan; 5. empeso; 6. ayegásh; 7. lavoras

Lesson 3

A. 1. estás; 2. estó; 3. está; 4. es; 5. está; 6. es; 7. estamos; 8. so; 9. estó; 10. estás; 11. es; 12. está; 13. somos; 14. es; 15. está

B. 1. Me plaze el livro. 2. Le agrada Yerushalayim. 3. Te agrada el muzeo. 4. Le plazen sus elevos. 5. Mos plazen muestros amigos.

6. Vos plaze Israel. 7. Vos agradan vuestros inyetos. 8. No me plaze estudiar. 9. No le plaze su médiko. 10. A mis djenitores no les plaze mi novio.

C. 1. tres ermanos; 2. una ermana; 3. vente parientes; 4. sesh oteles; 5. mueve amigos; 6. diziocho elevos

LESSON 4

A. 1. kome; 2. meto; 3. keren; 4. devemos; 5. komésh; 6. keres; 7. eskrivo; 8. mete; 9. komemos; 10. valen; 11. vende

B. 1. Este kayisí es savrozo. 2. Esta mansana es grande. 3. Akeyas prunas son buenas. 4. Yo komo esta fruta. 5. Esta sivdad es grande. 6. Mete la komanya en estos sakos. 7. Siempre merko la komanya en este pazar. 8. Kero estos tomates.

C. Prefero, prefere, prefere, preferimos, preferísh, preferen
Vendo, vendes, vende, vendemos, vendésh, venden
Meto, metes, mete, metemos, metésh, meten

D. Ventitres prunas; kuarenta i sinko mansanas; trenta i tres sakos; sesenta i siete kayisís; sinkuenta i dos portokales

LESSON 5

A. Lava!; Kanta!; Ven!; Melda!; Pika!; Korta!; Vende!; Eskrive!; Kome!; Di!

B. 1. Lávate las manos! 2. Eskrive tu nombre! 3. Korta las safanorias! 4. Munda patatas! 5. Melda este livro! 6. Kome las dulsuras! 7. Dame sal!

C. 1. El livro está sovre la meza. 2. Las patatas están en la chanta. 3. La chanta está debasho de la meza. 4. Veo a una ijika. 5. Veo dos livros. 6. Lava a este pekenyo ijiko. 7. Lava este findján. 8. Ayde kon mi al Pazar! 9. Este ombre es de Izmir.

LESSON 6

A. 1. aze; 2. ay; 3. ay; 4. aze; 5. aze; 6. ay

B. 1. Ke tiempo aze oy? 2. Aze frío i ay aire. 3. I akí aze kayente i seko. 4. Aze luvia. 5. Aze inyeve. 6. Empesa una borraska. 7. El sielo es grizo i enuvlado. 8. No aze luvia. 9. No me agrada kalor.

C. 1. En la kaza ay munchas odas. 2. En la sala ay muncho aire. 3. Ay muncho tiempo. 4. En ke sezón estamos? 5. Estamos en otonyo. 6. No aze kayente, el sielo es enuvlado i aze luvia. 7. Mandalde mis saludos a vuestros djenitores.

D. These are open-ended questions; many answers are possible.

E. 1. munchos portokales; 2. munchas mansanas; 3. muncho tiempo; 4. muncha inyeve; 5. munchas chantas; 6. munchos pipinos.

LESSON 7

A. 1. vo; 2. azes; 3. viene; 4. vengo; 5. saves; 6. vamos; 7. saven; 8. aze; 9. tenésh; 10. sé

B. 1. Sé avlar en evreo. 2. Saves ekrivir en espaniol? 3. Ke dizes? 4. Digo ke lo ago solo oy. 5. Eya va a azerlo oy. 6. Empesamos a freyir birmuelos. 7. Vamos a freyir birmuelos. 8. Eyos empesan a selebrar Hanuka. 9. Eyos van a selebrar Hanuka. 10. Ago un vestido para Purim. 11. Vo a azer un vestido para Purim. 12. Empeso a azer un vestido para Purim. 13. Eya dize ke va a ayudarme. 14. Ande vas? 15. Donde viene eya? 16. Ken va a venir?

Lesson 8

A. 1. La otra komida es menos savroza ke esta. 2. La sopa es mas kayente ke el gizado. 3. El otro livro es mas importante ke este. 4. Tu lugar es peor ke el mío.

B. Tengo meldado, tengo avierto, me tengo topado
Tienes meldado, tienes avierto, te tienes topado
Tiene meldado, tiene avierto, se tiene topado
Tenemos meldado, tenemos avierto, mos tenemos topado
Tenésh meldado, tenésh avierto, vos tenésh topado
Tienen meldado, tiene avierto, se tienen topado

C. 1. Tu ijo es mayor ke el mío. 2. El es mas alto de mi ermano. 3. Este muzeo es minor ke el Metropolitan. 4. Este merkato es menos karo ke el Pazar sentral. 5. Frutas son mas dulses de las vedruras. 6. Una mansana es tan savroza komo un kayisí. 7. El es mi mijor elevo. 8. Mi tío es mas viejo de mi tía. 9. Este es el peor día de mi vida. 10. Eya es la mijor kantadera ke tengo sintido. 11. La kantiga mueva es mas ermoza ke la vieja. 12. Este lugar es mijor ke akel. 13. Eya es tan godra komo él.

Lesson 9

A. 1. Laví las prasas. 2. Eya merkó las patatas. 3. Meldí una poemika. 4. Arrekojimos una koleksión grande de kantigas sefardís. 5. Fuetes al muzeo ayer? 6. Kijo sintir múzika djudeo-espanyola. 7. Mi famiya vino de Turkía. 8. Vinimos a una kazika. 9. Una morenika kantó una romansa. 10. La romansa fue en ladino.

B.

pertenesí	dividí	kompozí
pertenesites	dividites	kompozates
pertenesió	dividió	kompozó
pertenesimos	dividimos	kompozimos
pertenesitesh	dividitesh	kompozatesh
pertenesieron	dividieron	kompozaron

C. 1. chikitiko; 2. livriko; 3. kantigika; 4. kandelika; 5. ojiko;
6. kafeziko;

D. 1. grasioza; 2. ija; 3. saludo; 4. roza; 5. kuzina; 6. prasas;
7. savrozas

LESSON 10

A. konkistada; eskritos; merkadas; ekspulsados; avierta; meldados

B. 1. Los djudíos fueron ekspulsados de Espania en 1492. 2. Algunos de los ekspulsados fueron bien resividos en Portugal. 3. Mas tadre eyos fueron ekspulsados de aí también. 4. Eyos eskaparon a varias rejiones del Mediterraneo. 5. Algunos fueron bien aseptados en el Imperio Otomano. 6. Esta sivdad fue fundada en 1703 i fue yamada S. Petersburgo. 7. Eya fue fundada en la tierra resién konkistada.

C.

konkistava	ayudava	pertenesía	arresivía
konkistavas	ayudavas	pertenesías	arresivías
konkistava	ayudava	pertenesía	arresivía
konkistávamos	ayudávamos	pertenesíamos	arresivíamos
konkistavash	ayudavash	pertenesíash	arresivíash
konkistavan	ayudavan	pertenesían	arresivían

D. 1. Dos egzersisios fueron eskritos por eya. 2. Aleksandria fue fundada por Aleksandro el Grande. 3. Los djudíos fueron kombidados por Bayazid II. 4. La puerta fue avierta por ti.

LESSON 11

A. 1. El irá a Yerushalayim. 2. Mozotros meldaremos en ladino.
3. Venré del Saray a Saloniko. 4. Kuando komerás? 5. Komo te akseptarán ayí? 6. Vozotros sinyarésh la resevida. 7. Eya kantará en evreo.

B. 1. Voltaremos amaniana. 2. Eya va a volver adientro de dos oras.
3. Después tornarás a la eskierda. 4. Eyos ayegarán a las sinko.
5. Kantarásh en ladino? 6. Amaniana iremos al muzeo.
7. Después de esto vo a eskrivir una karta.

C. | | | | | | |
|---|---|---|---|---|---|
| sinyaré | perderé | partiré | merkaré | iré | seré |
| sinyarás | perderás | partirás | merkarás | irás | serás |
| sinyará | perderá | partirá | merkará | irá | será |
| sinyaremos | perderemos | partiremos | merkaremos | iremos | seremos |
| sinyarésh | perderésh | partirésh | merkarésh | irésh | serésh |
| sinyarán | perderán | partirán | merkarán | irán | serán |

LESSON 12

A. 1. dime; 2. kante; 3. aprendamos; 4. vengan; 5. venga

B. 1. No eskrivas! 2. No eskrivásh! 3. No komásh! 4. No vengas!
5. Eskrive! 6. Komed! 7. Avre tu livro! 8. No avras tu livro!

C. 1. No seas tonto/bovo! 2. No kantésh esta kantika! 3. Ven
a tiempo! 4. Aprende este refrán! 5. Avlad ladino! 6. No
avlésh turko.

LESSON 13

A. 1. merkó; 2. tengo; 3. merkaré; 4. veamos; 5. está; 6. bive

B. 1. Vo a Paris. 2. Akí están mi bilieto i pasaporte. 3. Onde
podemos rejistrar muestro bagaje? 4. Tengo una validja i una
chanta. 5. Onde está la salida número dodje? 6. Ke vuelo están
anunsiando? 7. Estás siguro ke esto está aí? 8. Eya está kontenta
de vervos. 9. El tiene aprendido muncho durante estos días.
10. Estamos kontentos ke mos veamos otra ves. 11. Tengo sed,
eya tiene ambre. 12. A la derecha está el muevo muzeo. 13. A la
eskierda está un restaurante.

C.

ponga	aga	sepa	venga
pongas	agas	sepas	vengas
ponga	aga	sepa	venga
pongamos	agamos	sepamos	vengamos
pongásh	agásh	sepásh	vengásh
pongan	agan	sepan	vengan

D. 1. Dudo ke el tiempo sea bueno. 2. Eya no duda ke el livro es interesante. 3. Kero ke tu vengas a tiempo. 4. Mi nono kere ke yo ambeze algunos refranes. 5. Eyos no kreen ke avlemos ladino. 6. Tu krees ke eya kanta muy bien.

Ladino-English Glossary
Vokabulario Ladino-Inglez

Note: This glossary does not include all meanings of the words or all variants.

adelantre forward
adío good-bye
adjustar add
adulterio *(m.)* adultery
aeroporto *(m.)* airport
agora now
agosto August
agradavle pleasant
agradeser to thank
aí there
ainda yet, still
aire *(m.)* air, wind
akí here
akompaniar, akompanyar to accompany
akonsejar to advise
akordarse (akodrarse, arrekodrar, arrekordar) to remember
akseptar to accept
aksión *(f.)* action
alguno one, some *(ind. adj.)*
alhad *(Ar.)* Sunday
alta tall
amaniana tomorrow
amargo bitter
amator *(m.)* amateur
ambezar to learn, to study, to teach
ambre *(f.)* hunger
amerikano *(m.)*, amerikana *(f.)* American
amigo *(m.)* friend

amo *(m.)* boss, owner
amor *(m.)* love
amostrar to demonstrate, to show
antepasado *(m.)* ancestor
antigo ancient
anunsiar to announce
anyo *(m.)* year
aparar to display the bride's trousseau
aparejar to prepare
aprender to learn
apresiar to appreciate
árabo Arab/Arabic
arkivo *(m.)* archive
armada *(f.)* army
arrekojer to collect, to gather
arresevir (resivir) to receive
artezano *(m.)* craftsman, artisan
asentarse to sit down
ashugar *(m.)* trousseau *(what a bride prepares for herself— clothing, bed, table linens, etc.)*
asperar to wait
aver to have *(only used as aux. v.)*
avierta *(adj.)* open
avión *(m.)* airplane
avlar speak, talk
avokato *(m.)*, avokata *(f.)* lawyer
avril April
avrir to open
ay there is, there are
ayá there

ayde *(T.)* let's go
ayegar to arrive, to come
ayer yesterday
ayudar to help
ayudo *(m.)* help
azeite *(m.)* olive oil
azer to do, to make

bagaje *(m.)* luggage
baklavá *(f.)* baklavá, Turkish
    sweetmeat
barato cheap
bashustoné *(T.)* with pleasure
bastante enough, quite, rather
batalia *(f.)* battle
Beit Ha-Tfutzot Museum of the
    Diaspora in Israel
bendisión *(f.)* benediction
berendjena *(f.)* eggplant
bever to drink
bezo *(m.)* kiss
bíbliko Biblical
bien *(adv.)* well
bilieto *(m.)* ticket
birmuelo *(m.)* doughnut
bisavós, bisavuelos *(m. pl.)*
    forefathers, ancestors
bivir to live
blando tender
blanko white
bolsa *(f.)* bag
borraska *(f.)* thunderstorm
bovo stupid
bueno *(adj.)* good
bushkar to search, to look for

chanta *(f., T.)* bag
chiko little, small

de *(prep.)* of, from
debasho de *(prep.)* under
dedikado dedicated

dedikar to dedicate
delantre de/enfrente de *(prep.)* in
    front of
derecha *(f.)* right *(direction)*
desembre December
deshar to leave, to let *(+ inf. s.o.
    do s.th.)*
deskonto *(m.)* discount
despozorio *(m.)* engagement
después after
destakarse to stand out
desvelopamiento *(m.)* development
dever must, have to, should
día *(m.)* day
dialekto *(m.)* dialect
diferensia *(f.)* difference
diferente different
difísil difficult
Dio *(m.)* God
distingir to distinguish, to define
diverso diverse
dividir to divide
dizer/dezir to say
djénero *(m.)* genre
djenitores *(m. pl.)* parents
djente *(f.)* people
djeográfiko geographic
djidió/djudío Jewish
djueves Thursday
djugar to play
djulio July
djunio June
dokumento *(m.)* document
dolor *(m.)* pain
dota *(f.)* dowry consisting of
    money and/or estate
dudar to doubt
dulsura *(f.)* sweets
durante during

edad *(f.)* age
egzaktamente exactly
egzersisio *(m.)* exercise

eksplikar (esplikar) to explain
ekspozisión *(f.)* exhibit
ekspulsar to expel
El Imperio Otomano the Ottoman
Empire
elevo/a *(Fr.),* **estudiante** student
embarkar to embark
empesar to begin
en *(prep.)* in
endelantre further on
enero January
enfrente de/delantre *(prep.)* in
front of
enkaso *(m.)* cash
ensenianza *(f.)* education
enseniar/ensenyar to teach
ensima *(prep.)* above
entender to understand
entrar to enter
entre *(prep.)* between
enuvlado cloudy
enverano *(m.)* summer
epiko *(adj.)* epic
ermana sister
ermano brother
ermozo beautiful
eskierda/sierda *(f.)* left *(direction)*
esklavo *(m.)* slave
eskrivir to write
esnaf *(m., Ar.)* craftsman, artisan
Espania, Espanya Spain
espaniol, espanyol Spanish
espesial special
estar/ser to be
estasión *(f.)* station
estonses then
estudiante, elevo/a *(Fr.)* student

fábrika *(f.)* factory
faltar/azer falta to miss, lack
something
famiya *(f.)* family

fantástiko terrific, exciting
fevrero February
fiel faithful
fiesta *(f.)* party
filmo *(m.)* movie
final final
findján *(m., T.)* cup
flako thin
folklor *(m.)* folklore
folklóriko *(adj.)* folk
forma *(f.)* form
formarse to form
fresko fresh
freyir to fry
frío *(m. n./adj.)* cold
fruta *(f.)* fruit
fuente *(f.)* source
fuerte strong
fundar to found
fuyir to run away, to flee

galante gallant
giadera *(f.)* guide
gizado *(m.)* stew
gizar to cook
godro fat
grado *(m.)* degree
grande big
grasias *(f. pl.)* thanks
grego Greek
grizo gray
guerta *(f.)* orchard, garden
guezmo *(m.)* smell

hakim *(m., Ar.)* judge
halvadji *(m., T.)* vendor of sweets
hamal *(m., T.)* porter, errand boy
hamor *(m.)* donkey
hazino sick, ill

i and
ija *(f.)* daughter

ijika *(f.)* girl
ijiko *(m.)* boy
ijo *(m.)* son
importante important
indikar to indicate, to specify
inimigo *(m.)* enemy
inspirar to inspire
interesante interesting
invierno *(m.)* winter
inyeta *(m.)* granddaughter
inyeto *(f.)* grandson
inyevar to snow
inyeve/nieve *(f.)* snow
ir to go
israelí Israeli

kada each, every
kafé/kavé *(m.)* coffee
kafedji *(m., T.)* coffee shop owner
kafeterya *(f.)* cafeteria
kaji nearly
kalavasika *(f.)* squash
kale *(+ inf.)* must, it is necessary to
kalor *(f.)* heat
kampo *(m.)* field
kantadera *(f.)* singer
kantador *(m.)* singer
kantar to sing
kantiga/kantika *(f.)* song
karne *(f.)* meat
karo expensive, dear
kartas *(f. pl.)* cards
kashera *(f.)* cashier
katálogo *(m.)* catalog
kavalería *(f.)* chivalry
kavaliero *(m.)* knight
kayente hot
kayisí *(m.)* apricot
kaza *(f.)* house
kazado(m.)/**kazada** *(f.)* married
kazal *(m.)* village
kazamentera *(f.)* matchmaker

kazarse to marry
ke? what?
kemar to burn
ken? who?
kerer to want
klase *(f.)* class
koleksión *(f.)* collection
komanya *(f.)* supplies, food
kombidar to invite
komer to eat
komersio *(m.)* commerce
komida *(f.)* meal, food
komo how; like, as
kompetisión *(f.)* contest,
    competition
kompozar to compose
komprar/merkar to buy
komunidad *(f.)* community
kon with
konkistar to conquer
konosensia *(f.)* acquaintance
konosido *(m.)* known
konsejero *(m.)* adviser
konserto *(m.)* concert
kontado *(m.)* cash
kontar to tell
koplas *(f. pl.)* songs, ballads, poems
kortar to cut
kostumbre *(f.)* custom, tradition,
    rite
koza *(f.)* thing
kozer to cook
kozido *(m.)* stew
kreasión *(f.)* creativity
kreer to believe
kriatura *(f.)* child
kristiano *(m. n./adj.)* Christian
kualkier any
kualo? what? *(as in what color,
    degree, temperature, etc.)*
kuando when
kultura *(f.)* culture
kuzina *(f.)* kitchen

lana *(f.)* wool
lanu *(H.)* our
lavar to wash *(s.o./s.th.)*
lavarse to wash *(oneself)*
lavorar to work
lechuga *(f.)* lettuce
legumes *(m. pl.)* legumes
lentejas *(f. pl.)* lentils
linea *(f.)* line
lingua *(f.)* language, tongue
lista *(f.)* list
literario literary
livre free
livro *(m.)* book
lugar *(m.)* place, seat
lunes Monday
luvia *(f.)* rain
luviar to rain
luz *(f.)* light

ma but
madre *(f.)* mother
madrugada *(f.)* early morning, dawn
maestro *(m.)*/**maestra** *(f.)* teacher
mal badly
malato sick, ill
maldar *(m. n.)* religious school
malo/negro bad
mandar to send
manko/menos less
mansana *(f.)* apple
maraviya *(f.)* marvel
marido *(m.)* husband
maror *(H.)* bitter
marso March
martes Tuesday
mas more
mayo May
mayor bigger
mayoriya *(f.)* majority
mazal *(m., H.)* luck

médiko *(m.)*, médika *(f.)* medical doctor, physician
Mediterraneo *(m.)* the Mediterranean
meldar to read
menester *(m.)* need, necessity
menos/manko less
mentirozo false
merkador *(m.)* merchant
merkar/komprar to buy
mes *(m.)* month
meter/poner to put
meza *(f.)* table
miérkoles Wednesday
mijor better
mijorar to improve
minor smaller, lesser, younger
minuto *(m.)* minute
mirar to look
mizmo self, the same
moderno modern
moendiz *(m., T., Ar.)* engineer
monte *(m.)* mountain
morar to live *(in a place)*, to dwell
morena dark-skinned girl
moro *(m.)* Moor
mudar to change *(place)*, to move
muerte *(f.)* death
muevo/nuevo new
mujer *(f.)* woman, wife
muncho/mucho much, many
mundar to peel
mundo *(m.)* world
musafir *(m., T., Ar.)* guest
museo *(m.)* museum
mushteri *(m./f., T., Ar.)* customer
muy very
múzika *(f.)* music
muzulmán Muslim

nada nothing
naser to be born

nasido born
nasional national
nesesitar to need
no no, not
nombre *(m.)* name
nono/avuelo/papu grandfather
novembre November
novia *(f.)* fiancée, bride
novio *(m.)* fiancé, bridegroom
nuevo/muevo new
número *(m.)* number
nuve *(f.)* cloud

oda *(f., T.)* room
ofisio *(m.)* job, occupation, office
ofreser to donate, to give as a
    present, to offer
oktobre October
okupar to occupy
ombre *(m.)* man
onde/ande? where?
ora *(f.)* hour
organizar to organize
oriental oriental
orijinal original
otel *(m.)* hotel
otobús *(m.)* bus
otonyo *(m.)* autumn, fall
otro other, another
oy today

padre *(m.)* father
palavra *(f.)*/biervo *(m.)* word
papel *(m.)* paper
para for
parás *(f. pl., T.)* money
pariente *(m./f.)* relative
parte *(f.)* part
parter *(m.)* orchestra *(in a theater)*
partir to leave
partisipasión *(f.)* participation
pasado *(adj.)* past
pasaporte *(m.)* passport

patatas *(f. pl.)*/kartof *(m.)* potatoes
patria *(f.)* homeland
payiz *(m.)* country
pazar/merkato *(m.)* bazaar, market
pedaso *(m.)* piece
pedrer/perder to lose
pekenyo little, small
peki *(T.)* OK
pensar (en) to think *(about)*
peor worse
pera *(f.)* pear
perfekto perfect, excellent
perkurar de *(+ inf.)* to try to *(do
    s.th.)*
perteneser/pertenser to belong
pezar to weigh
pezgado heavy
pikar to chop
pipino *(m.)* cucumber
pishin soon
poder can, to be able to
poema *(m./f.)* poem
poezía *(f.)* poetry, verses
poko a little
poner/meter put
popular popular
portokal *(m./f.)* orange
posivle possible
prasas *(f. pl.)* leeks
preferir to prefer
pregunta *(f.)* question
premio *(m.)* prize, award
preparar to prepare
preservar to keep, to preserve
presto quickly
prima *(f.)* first cousin
primavera *(f.)* spring
primo *(m.)* first cousin
prinsesa *(f.)* princess
prinsipal main
prisoniero *(m.)* prisoner

privilejio *(m.)* privilege
produksión *(f.)* production
profesión *(f.)* profession
profesor *(m.)*/**profesora** *(f.)*
   professor
próksimo next, nearest
propajar to propagate
provar to try
proverbio *(m.)* proverb, saying
pruna *(f.)* plum
puerta *(f.)* door

raramente rarely
raro rare
rávano *(m.)* horseradish
raya *(f.)* lightning
rázimo *(m.)* **de uvas** a bunch of
   grapes
razón *(f.)* reason
refrán *(m.)* proverb, saying
regalo *(m. n.)* gift, present
regla *(f.)* rule, requirement
rejión *(f.)* region
rejistrar to register
relasión *(f.)* relation
relijión *(f.)* religion
remansarse to settle
renkontrarse to meet each other
resevida *(f.)* receipt
resién recent, recently
restorante *(m.)* restaurant
rey *(m.)* king
riko rich
romansa *(f.)* romance, ballad

safanoria *(f.)* carrot
sako *(m.)* bag
sala *(f.)* hall, room
salida *(f.)* departure, exit
salir to leave, to go out
saludo/saludos *(m.)* greeting/best
   wishes
Saray Sarajevo

saver to know, to learn
savrozo tasty. delicious
sed *(f.)* thirst
seko dry
selebrar to celebrate
semana *(f.)* week
semejante similar
sena *(f.)* dinner
sentir to listen, to hear
sentirse to feel oneself
sentro *(m.)* center
septembre September
ser/estar to be
servir to serve
sevoya *(f.)* onion
sezón *(f.)* season of the year
shabat Saturday
si yes
sielo *(m.)* sky
siempre always
sigente next, following
siglo *(m.)* century
siguridad *(f.)* security
siguro sure
siklo *(m.)* cycle
sílava *(f.)* syllable
sinyar to sign
sinyor (Sr.) Mr.
sinyora (Sra.) Mrs.
sira *(f.)* row
sivdad *(f.)* city
sol *(m.)* sun, sunshine
solo only, alone
sonido *(m.)* sound
sopa *(f.)* soup
sorpreza *(f.)* surprise
sovre about, regarding, concerning,
   on
suerte *(f.)* fate, luck
sultán *(m.)* sultan
sumo *(m.)* juice
svivón *(m., H.)*/**dreidel** *(m.,Y.)* top
   (spinning top)

tabló *(m.)* display board
tadre *(f.)* afternoon
también also, too
tanto so many, much
teatro *(m.)* theater
telefono *(m.)* telephone
tema *(m./f.)* theme
temperatura *(f.)* temperature
tener have
terdjuman *(m., T.)* translator
terminar to end, to finish
territorio *(m.)* territory
tesido *(m.)* fabric
tía *(f.)* aunt
tidjaret *(f., T.)* trade, commerce
tiempo *(m.)* time, weather
tierra *(f.)* land
tío *(m.)* uncle
típiko typical
tipo *(m.)* type, kind
todo *(adj.)/(m.)* all, every/everything
todos all, everybody, everything
tomat *(m.)* tomato
tomatada *(f.)* tomato paste
tonto *(adj.)* stupid
topar to find, to come across
toparse kon to come across *(s.o.)*, to run into *(s.o.)*
tornar to turn
traer to bring
tradisionalmente traditionally
tren *(m.)* train
treslado *(m.)* translation
trokar to change
turko Turk, Turkish

último last
un/una one
universidad *(f.)* university
uzar use
uzo *(m.)* custom

valer to cost
validja *(f.)* suitcase
vario various
vazío empty, deserted
vedrura *(f.)/***zarzavat** *(m., T.)* vegetable
vendedor *(m.)* vendor
vender to sell
venir to come
ventana *(f.)* window
ventura *(f.)* luck
ver to see
verdá/verdad *(f.)* truth
verdadero true
ves *(f.)* time *(an occurence)*
vestido *(m.)* dress, costume
viajar to travel
viaje *(m.)* travel
viejo old
viento/aire *(m.)* wind
viernes Friday
virtud *(f.)* virtue
vizino *(m.)* neighbor
voltar/volver to return
vuelo *(m.)* flight
vuestro your

ya already
yamar to call
yamarse to call oneself, to be called
yelado cold, frozen
yero/yerro *(m.)* error, mistake
yerva *(f.)* grass

zanadji/artezano/esnaf *(m., T./m./ m., Ar.)* craftsman, artisan
zarzavatchi *(T.)* vegetable seller
zona *(f.)* zone, region

English-Ladino Glossary
Vokabulario Inglez-Ladino

about *(prep.)* sovre
above *(prep.)* ensima
accept aseptar
accompany akompaniar,
  akompanyar
acquaintance konosensia *(f.)*
action aksión *(f.)*
add adjustar
adultery adulterio *(m.)*
advise akonsejar
adviser konsejero *(m.)*
after después
afternoon tadre *(f.)*
age edad *(f.)*
air aire *(m.)*
airplane avión *(m.)*
airport aeroporto *(m.)*
all, every *(adj.)* todo
alone solo
already ya
also, too también
always siempre
amateur amator *(m.)*
American amerikano *(m.)*,
  amerikana *(f.)*
ancestor antepasado, bisavó,
  bisavuelo *(m.)*
ancient antigo
and i
announce anunsiar
any kualkier
apple mansana *(f.)*
appreciate apresiar
apricot kayisí *(m.)*
April avril

Arab, Arabic árabo
archive arkivo *(m.)*
army armada *(f.)*
arrive ayegar
as komo
August agosto
aunt tía *(f.)*

bad malo, negro
badly mal
bag chanta *(f.)*, sako *(m.)*, bolsa *(f.)*
baklavá *(f.)* baklavá, Turkish
  sweetmeat
battle batalia *(f.)*
bazaar pazar *(m.)*
be ser, estar
be born naser
beautiful ermozo
begin empesar
believe kreer
belong perteneser, pertenser
benediction bendisión *(f.)*
better mijor
between *(prep.)* entre
biblical bíbliko
bigger mayor
bitter amargo, maror *(H.)*
book livro *(m.)*
born nasido
boss amo *(m.)*
boy ijiko *(m.)*
bride novia *(f.)*
bridegroom novio *(m.)*
bring traer

brother ermano *(m.)*
burn kemar
bus otobús *(m.)*
but ma
buy merkar, komprar

cafeteria kafeterya *(f.)*
call yamar
call oneself, to be called yamarse
can poder
cards kartas *(f. pl.)*
carrot safanoria *(f.)*
cash kontado *(m.)*, enkaso *(m.)*
cashier kashera
catalog katálogo *(m.)*
celebrate selebrar
center sentro *(m.)*
century siglo *(m.)*
change trokar
cheap barato
child kriatura *(f.)*
chivalry kavalería *(f.)*
chop pikar
Christian *(n./adj.)* kristiano *(m.)*
city sivdad *(f.)*
class klase *(f.)*
cloud nuve *(f.)*
cloudy enuvlado
coffee kavé *(m.) or* kafé
coffee shop owner kafedji *(m., T.)*
cold *(n./adj.)* frío
collect arrekojer
collection koleksión *(f.)*
come venir
come across *(s.o.)*, **bump into**
   (s.o.) toparse kon
commerce komersio *(m.)*
community komunidad *(f.)*
competition kompetisión *(f.)*
compose kompozar
concert konserto *(m.)*
conquer konkistar

cook *(v.)* kozer, gizar
cost valer
country payiz *(m.)*
cousin prima *(f.)*, primo *(m.)*
craftsman zanadji *(m., T.)*, artesano
   (m.), esnaf *(m., Ar.)*
creativity kreasión *(f.)*
cucumber pipino *(m.)*
culture kultura *(f.)*
cup findján *(m., T.)*
custom kostumbre *(f.)*
customer mushteri *(m./f.)*
cut kortar
cycle siklo *(m.)*

daughter ija *(f.)*
dawn madrugada *(f.)*
day día *(m.)*
death muerte *(f.)*
December desembre
dedicate dedikar
dedicated dedikado
degree grado *(m.)*
demonstrate amostrar
departure salida *(f.)*
development desvelopamiento *(m.)*
dialect dialekto *(m.)*
difference diferensia *(f.)*
different diferente
difficult difísil
dinner sena *(f.)*
discount deskonto *(m.)*
display board tabló *(m.)*
distinguish distingir
diverse diverso
divide dividir
do azer
doctor médiko *(m.)*, médika *(f.)*
document dokumento *(m.)*
donate ofreser
donkey hamor *(m., H.)*
door puerta *(f.)*

doubt *(v.)* dudar
doughnut birmuelo *(m.)*
dowry ashugar *(m.)*, dota *(f.)*
dress *(n.)* vestido *(m.)*
drink *(v.)* bever
dry *(adj.)* seko
during durante
dwell morar

each kada
eat komer
education ensenianza *(f.)*
eggplant berendjena *(f.)*
embark embarkar
empty vazío
end *(v.)* terminar
enemy inimigo *(m.)*
engagement despozorio *(m.)*
engineer moendiz *(m., T., Ar.)*
enough bastante
enter entrar
epic *(adj.)* épiko
error yero, yerro *(m.)*
escape eskapar
everything todo *(m.)*
exactly egzaktamente
exercise egzersisio *(m.)*
exhibit *(n.)* ekspozisión *(f.)*
exit *(n.)* salida *(f.)*
expel ekspulsar
expensive karo
explain eksplikar, esplikar

fabric tesido *(m.)*
factory fábrika *(f.)*
faithful fiel
fall (autumn) otonyo *(m.)*
false mentirozo
family famiya *(f.)*
fat godro
fate, luck suerte *(f.)*
father padre *(m.)*

February fevrero
feel *(well)* sentirse
fiancé novio *(m.)*
fiancée novia *(f.)*
field kampo *(m.)*
final final
find topar
Finish terminar
flee fuyir
flight vuelo *(m.)*
folk *(adj.)* folklóriko
folklore folklor *(m.)*
following, next sigiente
for para
form *(n.)* forma *(f.)*
form *(v.)* formarse
forward adelantre
found fundar
free livre
fresh fresko
Friday viernes
friend amigo *(m.)*
frozen yelado
fruit fruta *(f.)*
fry freyir
further on endelantre

gallant galante
gather arrekojer
genealogical djenealójiko
genre djénero *(m.)*
geographic djeográfiko
gift regalo *(m.)*
girl ijika *(f.)*
go ir
God Dio *(m.)*
good bueno
granddaughter inyeta *(f.)*
grandfather nono, avuelo, papu *(m.)*
grandson inyeto *(m.)*
grapes uvas *(f. pl.)*
grass yerva *(f.)*

gray grizo
Greek grego
green beans frijoles vedres *(m. pl.)*
greeting saludo *(m.)*
guest musafir *(m.)*
guide giadera *(f.)*

hall sala *(f.)*
have tener
heat kalor *(f.)*
heavy pezgado
help *(n.)* ayudo *(m.)*
help *(v.)* ayudar
here akí
homeland patria *(f.)*
horseradish rávano *(m.)*
hot kayente
hotel otel *(m.)*
hour ora *(f.)*
house kaza
how komo
hunger ambre *(f.)*
husband marido *(m.)*

important importante
improve mijorar
in *(prep.)* en
in front of *(prep.)* delantre de,
  enfrente de
indicate indikar
inspire inspirar
interesting interesante
invite kombidar
Israeli israelí

January enero
Jew djudío (djidió)
Jewish djudeo
job ofisio, lavoro *(m.)*
judge hakim *(m., Ar.)*
juice sumo *(m.)*

July djulio
June djunio

king rey *(m.)*
kiss bezo *(m.)*
kitchen kuzina *(f.)*
knight kavaliero *(m.)*
know, learn saver
known konosido *(m.)*

land tierra *(f.)*
language lingua *(f.)*
last último
lawyer avokato *(m.)*, avokata *(f.)*
learn ambezar, aprender
leave partir, salir, deshar, kitar
leeks prasas *(f. pl.)*
left *(direction)* eskierda, sierda *(f.)*
legumes legumes *(m. pl.)*
lentils lentejas *(f. pl.)*
less manko, menos
let deshar *(+ inf. s.o. do sth.)*
lettuce lechuga *(f.)*
light *(n.)* luz *(f.)*
lightning raya *(f.)*
like, as komo
line linea *(f.)*
list lista *(f.)*
listen, hear sentir
literary literario
little chiko, pekenyo
live *(in a place)* bivir, morar en
local lokal
look mirar
lose pedrer, perder
love *(n.)* amor *(m.)*
luck mazal *(m.)*, ventura *(f.)*,
  suerte *(f.)*
luggage bagaje *(m.)*

main prinsipal
majority mayoriya *(f.)*

make azer
man ombre *(m.)*
many muncho, mucho
March *(month)* marso
market merkato *(m.)*
married kazado *(m.)*, kazada *(f.)*
marry kazarse
marvel maraviya *(f.)*
matchmaker kazamentera *(f.)*
May *(month)* mayo
meal komida *(f.)*
mean *(v.)* signifikar
meat karne *(f.)*
Mediterreanean Sea *(Mar)*
 Mediterraneo *(m.)*
meet each other renkontrarse
merchant merkador *(m.)*
minute minuto *(m.)*
miss *(v.)* faltar, azer falta
Missus (Mrs.) sinyora *(Sra.)*
Mister (Mr.) sinyor *(Sr.)*
modern moderno
Monday lunes
money parás *(f. pl.)*
month mes *(m.)*
Moor moro *(m.)*
more mas
mother madre *(f.)*
mountain monte *(m.)*
move mudar
movie filmo *(m.)*
much muncho, mucho
music múzika *(f.)*
Muslim muzulmán
must dever; kale *(+ inf.)*

name nombre *(m.)*
national nasional
nearest próksimo
need, necessity menester *(m.)*
need *(v.)* nesesitar

neighbor vizino *(m.)*
nervous nervozo
new muevo, nuevo
no, not no
nothing nada
November novembre
now agora
number número *(m.)*

OK peki *(from T. pek iyi)*
occupy okupar
October oktobre
of de
offer ofreser
office ofisio *(m.)*
old viejo
olive oil azeite *(m.)*
on *(prep.)* sovre
one un, una
onion sevoya *(f.)*
only solo
open *(adj.)* avierta
open *(v.)* avrir
orange *(fruit)* portokal *(m./f.)*
orchard guerta *(f.)*
orchestra parter *(m.) (seat in a
 theater)*
organize organizar
oriental oriental
original orijinal
other otro
our lanu *(H.)*
owner amo *(m.)*

pain dolor *(m.)*
paper papel *(m.)*
parents djenitores
part parte *(f.)*
participation partisipasión *(f.)*
party fiesta *(f.)*
passport pasaporte *(m.)*
past *(n./adj.)* pasado

pear pera *(f.)*
peel mundar
people djente *(f.)*
perfect perfekto
piece pedaso *(m.)*
place lugar *(m.)*
play djugar
pleasant agradavle
plum pruna *(f.)*
poem poema *(m./f.)*
poetry *(f.)* poezía
popular popular
porter hamal *(m., T.)*
possible posivle
potatoes patatas *(f. pl)*, kartof *(m.)*
prefer preferir
prepare preparar, aparejar
preserve preservar
princess prinsesa *(f.)*
prisoner prisoniero *(m.)*
privilege privilejio *(m.)*
prize premio *(m.)*
production produksión *(f.)*
profession profesión *(f.)*
professor profesor *(m.)*,
    profesora *(f.)*
propagate propajar
proverb proverbio, refrán *(m.)*
put meter, poner

question pregunta, domanda *(f.)*
quickly presto

rain luvia *(f.)*; luviar *(v.)*
rare raro
rarely raremente
read meldar
reason razón *(f.)*
receipt resevida *(f.)*
receive resivir, arresevir
recent, recently resién
region rejión *(f.)*

register rejistrar
relation relasión *(f.)*
relative *(n.)* pariente *(m./f.)*
religion relijión *(f.)*
remember arrekodrar, arrekordar,
    akordarse (akodrarse)
restaurant restorante *(m.)*
return voltar, volver
right *(direction)* derecha *(f.)*
romance romansa *(f.)*
room sala *(f.)*, oda *(f., T.)*
row sira *(f.)* *(in a theater,*
    airplane, etc.)
rule regla *(f.)*

same mizmo
Sarajevo Saray
Saturday Shabat
say dizer/dezir
saying refrán *(m.)*
school *(religious)* maldar *(m.)*
search bushkar
season *(of the year)* *(n.)* sezón *(f.)*
security siguridad *(f.)*
see ver
self mizmo
sell vender
send mandar
September septembre
serve servir
settle remansarse
sick hazino, malato
sign *(v.)* firmar
similar semejante
sing kantar
singer kantadera *(f.)*, kantador *(m.)*
sister ermana *(f.)*
sit down asentarse
sky sielo *(m.)*
slave esklavo *(m.)*
small chiko, pekenyo

smaller minor
smell guezmo *(m.)*
snow inyeve *(f.)*, nieve *(f.)*;
    inyevar *(v.)*
so many/so much tanto
some *(indefinite adjective)* alguno
son ijo *(m.)*
song kantiga, kantika *(f.)*
soon pishin
sound sonido *(m.)*
soup sopa *(f.)*
source fuente *(f.)*
Spain Espania, Espanya
Spanish espaniol, espanyol
speak avlar
special espesial
spring *(season)* primavera *(f.)*
squash kalavasika *(f.)*
stand out destakarse
station estasión *(f.)*
stew kozido *(m.)*, gizado *(m.)*
strong fuerte
student elevo,-a, estudiante
study ambezar
stupid tonto; bovo
suitcase validja *(f.)*
sultan sultán *(m.)*
summer enverano *(m.)*
sun sol *(m.)*
Sunday alhad *(Ar.)*
supplies komanya *(f.)*
sure siguro
surprise *(n.)* sorpreza *(f.)*
sweets dulsura *(f.)*
syllable sílava *(f.)*

table meza *(f.)*
talk avlar
tall alta
tasty savrozo
teach enseniar, ensenyar

teacher maestro *(m.)*, maestra *(f.)*
telephone telefono *(m.)*
tell kontar
temperature temperatura *(f.)*
tender blando
terrific fantástiko
territory territorio *(m.)*
thank agradeser
thanks grasias *(f. pl.)*
theater teatro *(m.)*
theme tema *(m./f.)*
then estonses
there aí, ayá
thin flako
thing koza *(f.)*
think *(about)* pensar (en)
thirst sed *(f.)*
thunderstorm borraska *(f.)*
Thursday djueves
ticket bilieto *(m.)*
time tiempo *(m.)*
time *(an occurence)* ves *(f.)*
today oy
tomato tomat *(m.)*
tomato paste tomatada *(f.)*
tomorrow amaniana
tongue língua *(f.)*, idioma *(m./f.)*
top *(n.)* svivón *(m., H)*, dreidel *(m., Y.)*
trade tidjaret *(f., T.)*
train tren *(m.)*
translation treslado *(m.)*
translator terdjuman *(m., T.)*
travel *(n.)* viaje *(m.)*
travel *(v.)* viajar
true verdadero
truth verdá, verdad *(f.)*
try provar, perkurar de *(+ inf.)*
Tuesday martes
Turk turko
turn tornar
type *(n.)* tipo *(m.)*
typical típiko

uncle tío *(m.)*
under *(prep.)* debasho de
understand entender
university universidad *(f.)*
use uzar

various vario
vegetable vedrura *(f.)*, zarzavat
(m., T.)
vendor vendedor *(m.)*
vendor of sweets halvadji *(m., T.)*
very muy
village kazal *(m.)*
virtue virtud *(f.)*

wait asperar
want kerer
wash lavar *(s.o./s.th.)*; lavarse
(oneself)
weather tiempo *(m.)*
Wednesday miérkoles
week semana *(f.)*
weigh pezar
well *(adv.)* bien
what? ke?

what? kualo? *(what color, degree,
temperature, etc.)*
when? kuando?
where? onde? ande?
who? ken?
wife mujer *(f.)*
wind viento, aire *(m.)*
window ventana *(f.)*
winter invierno *(m.)*
with kon
woman mujer *(f.)*
wool lana *(f.)*
word palavra *(f.)*
work *(v.)* lavorar
world mundo *(m.)*
worse peor
write eskrivir
year anyo *(m.)*
yes si
yesterday ayer
yet ainda
you tu, vozotros, vos
your vuestro

zone zona *(f.)*

APPENDIX I: Kondjugasión de los verbos regulares / Conjugation of Regular Verbs

The following chart contains conjugations of the three types of regular verbs that occur in Ladino—verbs ending in -ar, -er, and -ir—in the present tense, present perfect tense, simple past tense, the imperfect tense, the future tense of the indicative, and the present of the subjunctive.

verbo *Verb*	presente *Present*	presente perfekto *Present Perfect* [aver or tener + *past participle*]	pasado semple (pretérito) *Simple Past*	imperfekto *Imperfect*	futuro *Future*	presente de subjuntivo *Present Subjunctive*
I. Regular –ar Verbs						
I. kantar *to sing*	kanto kantas kantar kantamos kantásh kantan	*pres. tense of* aver or tener + kantado	kantí kantates kantó kantimos kantatesh kantaron	kantava kantavas kantava kantavámos kantavash kantavan	kantaré kantarás kantará kantaremos kantarésh katarán	kante kantes kante kantemos kantésh kanten
II. Regular –er Verbs						
II. komer *to eat*	komo komes kome komemos komésh komen	*pres. tense of* aver or tener + komido	komí komites komió komimos komitesh komieron	komía komías komía komíamos komiash komian	komeré komerás komerá komeremos komerésh komerán	koma komas koma komamos komásh koman

APPENDIX I: Kondjugasión de los verbos regulares / Conjugation of Regular Verbs
(Continued)

Plazer—to like—conjugates as a regular **–er** verb but is used primarily in the third person, singular and plural. The personal pronouns, **me, te, se,** etc., precede the verb as indirect objects. For example, to say *I like it* and *we like them,* the construction is **me plaze** and **mos plazen** (literally, *it is pleasing to me* and *they are pleasing to us*).

verbo *Verb*		presente *Present*	presente perfekto *Present Perfect* [aver *or* tener + *past participle*]	pasado semple (pretérito) *Simple Past*	imperfekto *Imperfect*	futuro *Future*	presente de subjuntivo *Present Subjunctive*
plazer *to like*	me te se mos vos se	plaze/plazen	*3ʳᵈ p.s. & pl. of* aver *or* tener + plazido	plazó/plazieron	plazía/plazian	plazerá/plazerán	plaza/plazan

III. Regular –*ir* Verbs

| **III. bivir**
to live | bivo
bives
bive
bivimos
bivish
biven | *pres. tense of*
aver *or* tener
+ bivido | biví
bivites
bivió
bivimos
bivitesh
bivieron | bivía
bivías
bivía
bivíamos
bivíash
bivían | biviré
bivirás
bivirá
biviremos
bivirésh
bivirán | biva
bivas
biva
bivamos
bivásh
bivan |

APPENDIX II: Kondjugasión de los verbos refleksivos / Conjugation of Reflexive Verbs

verbo *Verb*	presente *Present*	presente perfekto *Present Perfect* [aver or tener + past participle]	pasado semple (pretérito) *Simple Past*	imperfekto *Imperfect*	futuro *Future*	presente de subjuntivo *Present Subjunctive*
yamarse *to be named, to call oneself*	me yamo te yamas se yama mos yamamos vos yamásh se yaman	me, te, se, mos, vos, se before *pres. tense of* aver or tener + yamado	me yamí te yamates se yamó mos yamimos vos yamatesh se yamaron	me yamava te yamavas se yamava mos yamávamos vos yamavash se yamavan	me yamaré te yamarás se yamará mos yamaremos vos yamarésh se yamarán	me yame te yames se yame mos yamemos vos yamésh se yamen

APPENDIX III: Kondjugasión de verbos irregulares / Conjugation of Irregular Verbs

In various dialects of Ladino, there are diverse forms of the irregular verbs; some verbs may be regular in one dialect and irregular in others. Included in the following charts are some of the most common irregular verbs; you will note that some irregular verbs can be regular in one tense and irregular in another. Note that only the irregular conjugations of each verb are in boldface while the regular conjugations are in plain face.

The future tense of these verbs is not given because the forms of the verb stem to which the future tense endings (**-é, -ás, -á, -emos, -ésh, -án**) are added may vary according to dialect. For example, the verb-stem for **poder** *can, to be able to* may be **poder-, puedr-, podr-, pueder-**. It is beyond the scope of this book to list all future verb-stem variants that occur in all dialects.

Aver is only used as an auxiliary verb in compound tenses. Only the present tense of **aver** is given since the only compound tense introduced in this book is the present perfect, which is formed by using the present tense of **aver** plus the past participle of the main verb.

verbo *Verb*	presente *Present*	presente perfekto *Present Perfect* [aver *or* tener + *past participle*]	pasado semple (pretérito) *Simple Past*	imperfekto *Imperfect*	presente de subjuntivo *Present Subjunctive*
aver *auxiliary* *verb only*	**a/ave** **as/aves** **a/ave** **amos/avemos** **ash/avésh** **an/aven**				

*Irregular conjugations are in boldface.

azer
to do, make

ago	*pres. tense of* azía	**ize**	aga
azes	aver *or* tener azías	**izites**	agas
aze	+ **echo** azía	**izo**	aga
azemos	azíamos	**izimos**	agamos
azésh	azíash	**izitesh**	agásh
azen	azían	**izieron**	agan

dezir/dizer
to say

digo	*pres. tense of* dezía	**dishe**	diga
dizes	aver *or* tener dezías	**dishites**	digas
dize	+ **dicho** dezía	**disho**	diga
dizimos	deziamos	**dishimos**	digamos
dizísh	deziash	**dishitesh**	digásh
dizen	dezían	**disheron**	digan

estar
to be
located

estó	*pres. tense of* estava	**estuve**	**esté**
estás	aver *or* tener estavas	**estuvites**	**estés**
está	+ estado estava	**estuvo**	**esté**
estamos	estávamos	**estuvimos**	**estémos**
estásh	estavash	**estuvesh**	**estésh**
están	estavan	**estuvieron**	**estén**

ir
to go

vo	*pres. tense of* iva	**fui/fue**	**vaiga**
vas	aver *or* tener ivas	**fuetes**	**vaigas**
va	+ ido iva	**fue**	**vaiga**
vamos	ívamos	**fuemos**	**vaigamos**
vash	ivash	**fuetesh**	**vaigásh**
van	ivan	**fueron**	**vaigan**

APPENDIX III: Kondjugasión de verbos irregulares / Conjugation of Irregular Verbs

(Continued)

*Irregular conjugations are in boldface.

verbo / Verb	presente / Present	presente perfekto / Present Perfect [aver or tener + past participle]	pasado semple (pretérito) / Simple Past	imperfekto / Imperfect	presente de subjuntivo / Present Subjunctive
kerer to want	kero keres kere keremos kerésh keren	*pres. tense of* aver or tener + kerido	**kije kijites kijo kijimos kijitesh kijeron**	kería kerías kería keríamos keríash kerían	kera keras kera keramos kerásh keran
poder can, to be able to	**puedo**/podo **puedes**/podes **puede**/pode **puedemos**/podemos **puedésh**/podésh **pueden**/poden	*pres. tense of* aver or tener + podido	**pude/pode pudetes/podetes pudo/podo pudimos/podimos puditesh/poditésh puderon/poderon**	podía podías podía podíamos podíash podían	pueda/poda puedas/podas pueda/poda puedamos/podamos puedásh/podásh puedan/podan
saver to know	**sé** saves save savemos savésh saven	*pres. tense of* aver or tener + savido	**supe supetes supo supimos supitesh supieron**	savía savías savía savíamos savíash savían	**sepa sepas sepa sepamos sepásh sepan**

ser *to be*	so/sé sos es somos/semos sosh son	*pres. tense of* aver *or* tener + sido	fui/fue fuetes fue fuemos fuetesh fueron	era eras era éramos erash eran	sea seas sea seamos seásh sean
tener *to have*	tengo tienes tiene tenemos tenésh tienen	*pres. tense of* aver *or* tener + tenido	tuve tuvites tuvo tuvimos tuvitesh tuvieron	tenía tenías tenía teníamos teníash tenían	tenga tengas tenga tengamos tengásh tengan
venir *to come*	vengo vienes viene venimos venísh vienen	*pres. tense of* aver *or* tener + venido	vine vinites vino vinimos vinitesh vinieron	venía venías venía veníamos veníash venían	venga vengas venga vengamos vengásh vengan

Web Sites in or about Ladino

http://www.sephardicstudies.org/

https://jewishstudies.washington.edu/sephardic-studies/about-the-sephardic-studies-program/

http://arch.oucs.ox.ac.uk/detail/92234/index.html

http://www.orbilat.com/Languages/Spanish-Ladino/index.html

http://savethemusic.com/homepage-2/ (Ladino music and other Jewish folk music)

http://ladinokomunita.tallerdetinoco.org/

https://groups.yahoo.com/neo/groups/Ladinokomunita/info (Yahoo group for correspondence in Ladino)

http://esefarad.com/

https://lad.wikipedia.org/wiki/La_Primera_Hoja (Wikipedia in Ladino)

https://www.myjewishlearning.com/article/ladino-today/

https://www.avotsefarad.net/

http://legadosefardi.blogspot.com/

https://www.facebook.com/www.besepharad.net/

http://www.legadosefardi.net/

http://www.proyectos.cchs.csic.es/sefardiweb/node/10

The following is not a website, rather an article stating important fact — RAE (Spanish Royal Academy) creates a Judeo-Spanish branch:

https://www.theguardian.com/world/2017/aug/01/spain-honours-ladino-language-of-jewish-exiles

Audio Track List

Audio files available for download at:
http://www.hippocrenebooks.com/beginners-online-audio.html

FOLDER ONE

1. Title
2. Alphabet and Pronunciation
3. Stress
4. Les 1 Conversation
5. Les 1 Conversation for repetition
6. Les 1 Vocabulary
7. Les 1 Expressions
8. Les 2 Conversation
9. Les 2 Conversation for repetition
10. Les 2 Vocabulary
11. Les 2 Expressions
12. Les 3 Conversation
13. Les 3 Conversation for repetition
14. Les 3 Vocabulary
15. Les 3 Expressions
16. Les 3 Cardinal Numbers
17. Les 4 Conversation
18. Les 4 Conversation for repetition
19. Les 4 Vocabulary
20. Les 4 Cardinal Numbers
21. Les 5 Conversation
22. Les 5 Conversation for repetition
23. Les 5 Vocabulary
24. Les 5 Expressions
25. Les 6 Conversation
26. Les 6 Conversation for repetition
27. Les 6 Vocabulary
28. Les 6 Expressions
29. Les 7 Conversation
30. Les 7 Conversation for repetition
31. Les 7 Vocabulary
32. Les 7 Hebrew and Yiddish words
33. Les 7 Days of the week
34. Les 7 Months
35. Les 7 Expressions

FOLDER TWO

1. Les 8 Conversation 1
2. Les 8 Conversation 1 for repetition
3. Les 8 Conversation 2
4. Les 8 Conversation 2 for repetition
5. Les 8 Vocabulary
6. Les 8 Expressions
7. Les 9 Conversation
8. Les 9 Conversation for repetition
9. Les 9 Vocabulary
10. Les 9 Expressions
11. Les 10 Conversation
12. Les 10 Conversation for repetition
13. Les 10 Vocabulary
14. Les 10 Expressions
15. Les 11 Conversation
16. Les 11 Conversation for repetition
17. Les 11 Vocabulary
18. Les 11 Expressions
19. Les 12 Conversation 1
20. Les 12 Conversation 1 for repetition
21. Les 12 Vocabulary
22. Les 12 Expressions
23. Les 13 Conversation 1
24. Les 13 Conversation 1 for repetition
25. Les 13 Vocabulary
26. Les 13 Expressions

Acknowledgements

Writing this book has been a difficult, and at the same time challenging, task as there are no unified variant or standard grammar books of the Ladino language. Nonetheless, the author is responsible for any mistakes or oversights.

A number of people have been helpful in bringing this manual to fruition and I would like to thank them. I am grateful to the editors Lynn Visson, Linda Saputelli and Mary Tahan whose expertise and precise attention to detail can be paralleled only by their patience. I am deeply indebted to Daisy Braverman, Ladino language copyeditor Rebecca Skolnik, Ben Aguado, and Albert N. Contente, Ladino readers, along with Ms. Braverman, for the CD recordings. The book has benefited from their comments and insights.

Finally, I am grateful to my husband who has encouraged and helped me in carrying out this difficult task, and our sons for their patience, understanding, and support during a time when I could not pay much attention to them.

Printed in the USA
CPSIA information can be obtained
at www.ICGtesting.com
JSHW011419230424
61724JS00016B/570